THE TEACH YOURSELF BOOKS
EDITED BY LEONARD CUTTS

BIBLE ATLAS

Uniform with this volume and in the same series

TEACH YOURSELF:
THE CHRISTIAN FAITH

TEACH YOURSELF:
CHRISTIAN THEOLOGY

THE TEACH YOURSELF
GUIDEBOOK TO THE BIBLE

TEACH YOURSELF:
PREACHING

TEACH YOURSELF
HEBREW

TEACH YOURSELF
NEW TESTAMENT GREEK

THE TEACH YOURSELF
NEW TESTAMENT IN MODERN ENGLISH

THE TEACH YOURSELF
HISTORY OF RELIGIONS

TEACH YOURSELF:
THE DEAD SEA SCROLLS

THE TEACH YOURSELF
BIBLE ATLAS

By
H. H. ROWLEY
M.A., D.D., F.B.A.
Emeritus Professor of Hebrew, University of Manchester

THE ENGLISH UNIVERSITIES PRESS LTD
102 NEWGATE STREET
LONDON E.C.1

First printed 1960

Text and illustrations printed by Butler & Tanner Ltd., Frome and London
Maps compiled and printed by George Philip & Son Ltd., London
Blocks by The Grout Engraving Co., Bromley, Kent

PREFACE

THE aim of this Teach Yourself book is to provide what the reader has come to expect of an Atlas of the Bible—maps, text, and illustrations. The maps have been prepared by Messrs. George Philip and Son, whose name is their best guarantee. The text treats briefly of the geography and history of the Bible and of the service of Near Eastern archaeology to the student of Scripture. Here my chief difficulty, in a work of this compass, has been to include as much as possible without loss of clarity and balance. The Plates have been gathered from a variety of sources, and I have tried to have them as varied as possible and to choose illustrations which would give the reader some impression of what Biblical places look like.

In the text of the book names are given in the form they have in the Revised Standard Version (generally agreeing with those of the Revised Version). On the maps the same forms have been given, but Hebrew emphatic letters have been indicated by diacritic marks. Question marks indicating doubtful identifications of sites have been used sparingly, but the reader should not assume that where there is no such mark the identification is certain. In the list of Map References I have given the modern name of the site with which the Biblical place is believed to be identified.

It is my hope that this Atlas will be found of service to students of the Bible and will quicken their interest in this greatest of books.

H. H. ROWLEY

Manchester
April 1960

ACKNOWLEDGEMENTS

(Numbers refer to Plates)

2: Canon J. Creten, Louvain, Belgium. 3, 5, 12, 14, 19: The Matson Photo Service, Los Angeles, U.S.A. 4: Professor P. Benoit, O.P., École Biblique et Archéologique Française, Jerusalem. 6, 8, 27; Paul Popper Ltd., London. 7: Elia Photo-Service, Jerusalem. 9, 23, 24: Willem Van de Poll, Amsterdam. 10: J. Glissenaar and P. Pennarts, Montfoort, Holland. 11, 13, 21, 25: L. H. Grollenberg, O.P., Nijmegen, Holland. 15: Caisse Nationale des Monuments Historiques, Paris. 16: Directorate General of Antiquities, Baghdad, Iraq. 17: The Mansell Collection, London. 20: S. J. Schweig, Jerusalem. 22: Keren Hayesod Archives, Jerusalem. 26: A. J. Van de Voort, S.C.J., Liesbosch, Holland. 28: Alinari, Rome.

ILLUSTRATIONS FROM BOOKS

1: *Atlas of the Bible* (English Edition), Thomas Nelson and Sons Ltd., 1956. 18: *The Lachish Letters*, *Volume I*, Oxford University Press, 1938 (by permission of the Trustees of the late Sir Henry S. Wellcome).

CONTENTS

LIST OF PLATES

LIST OF MAPS

—1—

The Geography of Palestine

EVERY nation's history is influenced by its geographical situation and character, though none is determined wholly by these things. It is not therefore surprising that attention to the geography of Palestine is essential for the understanding of the history which is recorded in the Bible.

Palestine lies at the south-western end of what Breasted called the " Fertile Crescent ", which runs from the Persian Gulf up the valleys of the Tigris and Euphrates and down the Mediterranean seaboard to the frontier of Egypt, with the great Arabian desert lying to the south. Hence Palestine itself lies on the line of communications joining Asia and Africa. In peace-time its roads have from time immemorial been traversed by traders passing from Egypt to Asia Minor and the Mesopotamian kingdoms or in the reverse direction, while in times of war armies have passed back and forth along the same roads, and the control of this narrow strip of land has been of great importance for the ambitions of many monarchs. It has never been the centre of a great empire or the home of a culture whose influence has spread throughout any large area. At no time has its language been widely used beyond its own borders. Yet it has exercised an influence on the world that is unique, and the adherents of three great religions count it holy. Here monotheism was born, to become the heritage not alone of Judaism but of Christianity and Islam.

In *size* this land is about the same as Wales, even when its total extent east and west of the Jordan is reckoned, and rarely in Biblical times was the whole of this area under a single government. Frequently its length from north to south is described in the Bible as " from Dan to Beersheba ". This is a distance of about 150 miles. In *character* this tiny land is surprisingly varied. The snow-capped Hermon (Plate 14), which lies just north of Dan, rises to a height of over 9,000 feet, while much of the Jordan valley is below sea level, and the surface of the Dead Sea is lower than any other part of the earth's surface. It is, indeed, nearly 1,300 feet below sea level, while the bottom of the Dead Sea lies a further 1,300 feet lower still.

The whole country falls into four parts:

1. The Coastal Plain. The coastline of Palestine is not marked by many inlets or bays, but is broken principally by the projection of Mount Carmel. In ancient times there were no good ports, and this in part explains why the Israelites were never a seafaring people. Such ports as there were had no good harbourage, and it was not until after the First World War that modern engineers gave the land its first real harbour.

North of Carmel there lies a small strip of the coastal plain, running round the bay from Acco to Carmel, but when the Israelites entered the land they did not get possession of Acco itself (Judges 1: 31), and this town does not figure in the story of Israel in Old Testament times. By its later name of Ptolemaïs it is mentioned in 2 Maccabees 13: 24 f. and in Acts 21: 7.

From Carmel to Joppa stretches the Plain of Sharon (Isa. 35: 2). This is not watered by perennial rivers, but it has more rainfall than the country farther south, and a remarkably low range of variation of temperature between night and day throughout the year. Its width is little more than twelve miles, and through it ran the principal route from the north to Egypt. Here armies marched for invasion or defence, and the people who dwelt among its fields and forests must often have experienced the disruption of war.

South of Joppa, running to the Egyptian border, lay the Philistine Plain. On its shores the Philistines landed early in the twelfth century B.C. to occupy this coastal region and ultimately to give their name to the whole land. For the name Palestine is derived from Philistine. Here lay the five cities of the Philistines, and from here Philistine influence spread up the Plain of Sharon until the time of David. Hence it was not merely the lack of harbours along the coast, but the uncertain access to the sea which Israel enjoyed, which effectively prevented her from becoming a seafaring folk. Despite its lower rainfall than that of the Plain of Sharon, this section of the coastal plain is better watered by streams, and provides good agricultural land.

2. The Hill Country. Farther inland than the coastal plain lies the range of hill country that forms the backbone of the land, and that is of primary interest to the student of the Bible. This is once more divided laterally into three parts, familiar to us as Galilee, Samaria, and Judah.

Galilee figures more in the New Testament than in the Old. Here Jesus was brought up at Nazareth (Plate 21), and much of His recorded ministry was exercised within its bounds. It is divided into two parts, Upper Galilee in the north and Lower Galilee in the south. Together they form the foothills of the Lebanon (Plate 13). Parts of Upper Galilee reach a height of more than 3,000 feet, and the highest peak is not far short of 4,000 feet high. Lower Galilee nowhere rises above 2,000 feet. It enjoys a milder climate and its soil is very productive. Through Galilee, not far from Nazareth, passed the main road from Damascus to the south, which later ran out to the coast road mentioned above.

Separating Galilee from the central highlands of Samaria is the Valley of Jezreel, or of Esdraelon. Here lay some of the cities which the Israelites were not able to take when they settled in the land, and here were fought some of the battles which figure in the Old Testament. From the hills on the southern side of the valley Saul led his troops to the fatal field of Gilboa. Farther west Megiddo and Taanach guarded the passes which led over to the coast road. Near Taanach was fought the battle against Sisera, which formed the subject of the triumphant Song of Deborah (Judges 5), while near Megiddo Josiah met his end in the encounter with Pharaoh Neco (2 Kings 23: 29). It is probable that the name of Megiddo is preserved in the word Armageddon (Rev. 16: 16). From very ancient times the position of Megiddo gave it special importance, and it is not surprising that when it came into Israelite hands it was maintained as a fortified city. Some of Solomon's chariots were kept here (1 Kings 9: 15), and modern excavations have uncovered what were almost certainly part of his stables. East of these cities lay Jezreel, which provided the name of the valley. In this city was Naboth's vineyard, coveted by Ahab and secured for him by the ruthless Jezebel (1 Kings 21), who later paid for her crime with her life in the same city (2 Kings 9: 30–37). On the northern side of the valley stood the solitary, round-topped hill of Tabor (Plate 22), where Deborah and Barak mustered their forces prior to the battle mentioned above. Tabor is not mentioned in the New Testament, but it is the traditional mount of the Transfiguration. From the west of the Valley of Jezreel the river Kishon flows out to the Mediterranean through the Plain of Acco. In this river, swollen by the heavy rain, many of Sisera's men perished. The streams which flow eastwards into the Jordan are not mentioned by name in the Bible.

South of the Valley of Jezreel lay the central highlands, the two most conspicuous peaks of which are Gerizim and Ebal (Plate 9), close by the ancient Shechem, the former not quite 3,000 feet high and the latter just over 3,000 feet. These mountains were regarded as sacred by the Israelites, but with the founding of the Temple in Jerusalem they became overshadowed in the southern tradition, which dominates the Old Testament. The Samaritans, however, in post-exilic days continued to hold them sacred, and built their Temple on Mount Gerizim, and in New Testament times, when Jesus spoke with the woman of Samaria, He was questioned about the rival claims of Jerusalem and Gerizim (John 4: 20). Shechem was an ancient and strong city, and here the northern tribes gathered at the time of the Disruption (1 Kings 12: 1). Later Omri created Samaria to be the capital of the northern kingdom (1 Kings 16: 24). Like Jerusalem, it was strong by position and not by art alone, and its long resistance to the arms of the Assyrians showed the wisdom of Omri's choice.

South of Shechem lay Shiloh, once the home of the Ark and the shrine kept by Eli (1 Sam. 4). The Danish excavations there showed that it was destroyed in the eleventh century B.C., doubtless by the Philistines after the capture of the Ark.

More isolated than the central highlands is the hill country of Judah. This lay off the main road from north to south, and this fact is reflected in the history of the country. It is separated from the central highlands by a belt of lower hill country, but farther south the hills rise once more to over 3,000 feet. By far the strongest city was Jerusalem, an old Jebusite city which was believed to be impregnable by the military resources of David, but which was captured by a ruse and made the capital of David's kingdom, and which continued to be the capital of the southern kingdom to the end of its history (Plate 7). As in the case of Samaria, its natural position was one of great strength.

Farther south lay Hebron, the highest city of Judah, associated in tradition with the patriarch Abraham and the seat of David during the early years of his reign (2 Sam. 2: 1–4). Here, too, Absalom raised the standard of revolt and rallied support (2 Sam. 15: 7 ff.), doubtless resting in part on hostility to the transfer of the seat of government to Jerusalem. Between Jerusalem and Hebron lay Bethlehem (Plate 19), the city where David was brought up and where Jesus was born. North of Jerusalem was Bethel, where was an ancient sanctuary associated with Jacob in tradition (Gen. 28: 10 ff.), which was later made one of the two royal sanctuaries of the northern kingdom. In the far south lay Beersheba, the southern limit of the land in its common definition.

West of the hill country of Judah was the lowland of Judah, or the Shephelah, bordering on the Philistine country. This was more productive than the rocky hill country, and here were a number of strong cities which figure in the history, such as Lachish and Azekah, the two cities which together with Jerusalem alone held out to the end against Nebuchadrezzar in 586 B.C. (Jer. 34: 7). To the east of the hill country lay the wilderness of Judah, bordering on the Dead Sea. Here in recent years have been found the famous Dead Sea Scrolls, emanating from a Jewish sect that had its centre in Qumrân from the second century B.C. to the time of the Jewish War against Rome in A.D. 66–70.

South of Judah is the Negeb, which stretches from Beersheba to Kadesh-barnea, in the neighbourhood of which the Israelites are said to have spent thirty-eight of the forty years in the wilderness. Here the meagre rainfall makes sustained cultivation difficult, save when there is irrigation from the outside, or very efficient water conservation. There is evidence that there have been times in the past when this was carried out, and in recent years Israeli measures have brought a new fruitfulness to large areas of the Negeb—a term which is now extended in meaning to cover the area stretching to Elath, on the Gulf of Aqaba.

3. The Jordan Valley. The Jordan valley is part of the great geological fault which runs from Syria down to the Red Sea. In the north it separates the Lebanon from Anti-Lebanon, while south of the Dead Sea it is continued in the Arabah. The sources of the river lie north of Dan, and south of Dan it flows into Lake Huleh, which is not mentioned in the Bible. Not far from Lake Huleh to the south lay Hazor, the city of Jabin, recently excavated by Dr. Yigael Yadin. Between Lake Huleh and the Sea of Galilee the waters fall rapidly, and by the time the river reaches the latter it is already 700 feet below sea level.

The Sea of Galilee (Plate 14) is really a lake, though in the Bible it is more often called a sea. In the Old Testament it is called the Sea of Chinnereth, and in the New it has the alternative names of the Sea of Tiberias and the Lake of Gennesaret. To readers of the New Testament it will always be associated with the ministry of Jesus, who preached in its villages and towns on both sides, and who sailed on its waters. In some parts the hills rise from the shores, and the winds that rush down the valleys cause the sudden storms that we read of in the Gospels. In New Testament times there was a flourishing fishing industry in the lake, and some of our Lord's disciples were engaged in fishing here before they followed Him. On the shores of the lake once stood Capernaum, which is now a ruined site, and Bethsaida and Chorazin, no longer securely identifiable. Farther south on the western side lay the fertile Plain of Gennesaret, and south again the city of Tiberias, now surviving in a small village. On the west of the Sea of Galilee, as farther north in the region of Lake Huleh, the flowers abound in the springtime, and the scene is one of great loveliness.

From the Sea of Galilee to the Dead Sea is a distance of little more than sixty miles, but the winding course of the river greatly multiplies its length (Plate 6). At the northern end lay a plain which links up with the Valley of Jezreel, and in which stood the ancient Beth-shan. At the southern end lay the broader plain in which Jericho stood. Recent excavations have shown that this was a very ancient city, perhaps the most ancient city in the world. Its climate is very hot, owing to its position so far below the sea level, and although its rainfall is meagre it is supplied by springs and is able to produce palm groves, where many kinds of dates may be produced. The road from Jerusalem to Jericho fell sharply and in places was wild and perilous, being the resort at times of such robber bands as the one that figures in the story of the Good Samaritan (Luke 10: 30 ff.).

Between the two plains mentioned above, the valley

of the Jordan is narrow and well-wooded, and wild animals infested it. It is this part that is referred to in Jeremiah 12: 5 as the jungle (R.V. pride) of Jordan (Plate 6). In the upper part of this section of the river the water is clear, but then it becomes a muddy stream, which excited the contempt of Naaman (2 Kings 5: 12).

The Dead Sea is fifty-three miles long and about ten miles wide. It contains so high a proportion of salt that no fish can live in it and it is impossible to sink in it. It has, indeed, six times the salt content of the ocean, and in recent years potash and other chemicals have been profitably extracted from its waters. It lies in an arid and desolate region, and on its western side stood the Herodian fortress of Masada, excavated by Israeli archaeologists, while on the eastern side stood the other fortress of Machaerus, first built by Alexander Jannaeus and later rebuilt by Herod, and the place where, according to Josephus, John the Baptist was imprisoned and beheaded. On the south-western side of the Dead Sea the peninsula known as the Tongue projects into the sea. In ancient times the sea was less extensive than it now is, and somewhere in this region stood the cities of the plain, which included Sodom and Gomorrah. The precise location of these cities can no longer be identified with certainty, and some scholars believe that they are now submerged beneath the waters of the sea.

From the Dead Sea to the Gulf of Aqaba lies the Arabah, a valley with an average width of about five miles, whose surface consists of loose stones and sand. It has scattered trees, but little enduring vegetation. Through this valley the Israelites passed during the period of the wandering in the wilderness. It rises to a height of more than 650 feet above sea level, and then descends to the Gulf of Aqaba. There were periods when

Israelite kings controlled this area, but it was never securely held by them for long. From Ezion-geber, on the Gulf of Aqaba, Solomon sent forth his ships on their trading enterprises, and near here he developed the copper mining and smelting of which we have knowledge from modern archaeological exploration, though not from the Bible.

4. Transjordan. The country west of the Jordan consists of a high plateau, rising to a height of nearly 4,000 feet, divided laterally by its main rivers. Of these there are four principal streams. In the north the Yarmuk, which is unmentioned in the Bible, flows into the Jordan a little below the Sea of Galilee. Farther south flows the Jabbok, beside which Jacob had his struggle with the angelic visitor (Gen. 32: 22 ff.). Flowing into the Dead Sea, about half-way down its eastern side, is the Arnon, flanked by sheer cliffs (Plate 4) along part of its course. Flowing into the southern end of the Dead Sea is the Zered, which like the Arnon runs through a deep gorge.

North of the Yarmuk lay Bashan, the kingdom of Og. It was assigned to part of the tribe of Manasseh, but played little part in the history of Israel after the Settlement. It was noted for its fierce cattle, and its soil was productive, though its rainfall was low.

Between the Yarmuk and the Jabbok lay the country of Gilead. Here stood Ramoth-gilead, Jabesh-gilead, Succoth, and Penuel, as well as other places that figure in the Old Testament, and most of the towns of the Decapolis, which is mentioned in the New.

From the Jabbok to the Arnon was the territory occupied by Gad and Reuben, with the Ammonite territory lying farther to the east. Reuben early fell into insignificance and disappeared from history. Almost level with the northern end of the Dead Sea stood Mount Nebo, the mountain from which Moses viewed the Promised Land (Plate 5), and where he died. South of the Ammonites were the Moabites, whose people were also found north of the Arnon as well as to the south. Dibon, where the Moabite Stone (Plate 15) was found, stands north of the Arnon, and north of that again Heshbon, the seat of the kingdom of Sihon, who was defeated by the incoming Israelites.

Between the Arnon and the Zered lay country which was assigned to Reuben, but which seems to have seen little effective occupation by that tribe. Ar and Kir-hareseth stood here, and these continued to be Moabite cities. South of the Zered lay the country of Edom, whose principal city, Sela or Petra, is famous for its rock-hewn ruins.

From this brief account it is clear that there were great obstacles to the unified control of this whole land. Its communications were hampered by natural barriers, and between Transjordan and the west of the Jordan were only possible at points where the river could be forded. Transjordan was exposed to incursions from the desert and had little protection, while the country west of the Jordan was involved in the struggles of the empires that lay to the north and the south, and through long periods of history was not allowed to live its own life unmolested.

—2—

The World of the Bible

WE must now turn our attention beyond the bounds of Palestine itself to look at the wider world whose history constantly affected the life of the inhabitant of Palestine. To the east lay the ancient civilization of Babylonia, and to the south the other ancient civilization of Egypt. According to Israelite tradition Abraham once lived in Ur of the Chaldees (Gen. 11: 31), and the Israelites for long years sojourned in Egypt, where they were put to task work (Plate 1). The kingdom of Assyria, which lay north of Babylonia, cherished the ambition to extend its rule to the Mediterranean, and finally engulfed the whole Mediterranean seaboard, to be displaced by the Neo-Babylonian empire under Nebuchadrezzar. Moreover, Israel was constantly at war with her nearer neighbours throughout the pre-exilic period. In the post-exilic period she was brought into the stream of the life of the yet more extensive Persian empire, and then of the empire of Alexander and the kingdoms that developed out of it, and finally of the Roman empire.

1. Babylonia. The earliest inhabitants of Babylonia of whom we have knowledge were the Sumerians. They attained a high degree of civilization, and invented the cuneiform system of writing which was later adopted for the Akkadian language. The Sumerians were not Semites, and their language was not a Semitic language. Moreover, their cuneiform signs represented ideas rather than sounds, and so were ideographic. When the Semitic Akkadians settled in Babylonia, they gave their name Akkad to the northern part of it. About 2350 B.C.

Sargon established the first Semitic dynasty in Babylonia, which became known as Sumer and Akkad. The Akkadians adapted the Sumerian signs to syllabic use, and in the course of time Babylon became their chief city. Sumer and Akkad lay along the lower reaches of the Tigris and the Euphrates, down to the Persian Gulf, whose northern end in ancient times reached much farther north than it does today. The Akkadian language and the signs whereby it was represented in writing were used in Assyria also, and they were simplified and adapted to alphabetic, instead of syllabic, use by the people of Ugarit, who will be mentioned below. That Babylonian influence extended far to the west is illustrated by the fact that the Amarna Letters, which were written in the fourteenth century B.C. by the Palestinian princes to their Egyptian overlord, were written in Akkadian.

2. Assyria. To the north of Babylonia lay Assyria, with its capital first at Ashur and later at Nineveh. But we have not to think of Babylonia and Assyria standing side by side through all periods and dividing between them the whole of Mesopotamia. In the second millennium B.C. the powerful kingdom of Mitanni lay between Assyria and the Hittite kingdom of Asia Minor. In early times the cities of Babylonia were independent cities which fought one another, so that now one and now another attained the greatest power. Farther north there were cities like the ancient Mari and Nuzu, living an independent life until brought within some wider kingdom, and a variety of peoples inhabited this whole area. The Hurrians, with a language of their own, whose influence is strongly seen at Nuzu, played a part in the struggles of these lands, and the Horites of the Bible are believed to belong to this people. The

Amorites, too, were once powerful in northern Mesopotamia. They were established at Mari, and they provided the First Dynasty of Babylon, to which Ḫammurabi belonged. Moreover, there were Aramaeans in Mesopotamia. We find them referred to in the Bible as inhabiting Aram-naharaim and Paddan-Aram, as well as Damascus. In Asia Minor were the Hittites, a non-Semitic people, with their capital at Hattushash, who used a hieroglyphic script of their own. Once a powerful people they spread their influence to Carchemish, on the Euphrates, and sought to press down into Syria and Palestine, until checked by Assyrian arms. Gradually, however, within the period of Israelite history after the settlement in Canaan, Assyria spread her power from the Tigris to the Mediterranean, and then through Syria, so that down to the rise of the Neo-Babylonian empire Assyria is the only Mesopotamian power which affected the Israelites. When the Assyrian empire fell before the Medes and the Chaldaeans, who by now had established their rule in Babylon and created the Neo-Babylonian empire, the Israelites soon came under their sway, and the exiles from the southern kingdom of Judah were carried away to Babylonia.

3. Egypt. The ancient civilization of Egypt grew up along the banks of the Nile, whose annual overflow of its banks is essential to the life of the country. It was divided into Upper Egypt and Lower Egypt, and in Hebrew the name of the country is a dual formation. The splendour of its civilization is evidenced by its great monuments, with their long and important inscriptions in the hieroglyphic script which is represented in the great museums of the world. Its influence waxed and waned, and under its more powerful monarchs spread to Palestine. In the fifteenth century B.C. Thothmes III made effective the Egyptian claim to this land, but in the following century Egyptian power in Palestine reached a low ebb. In the thirteenth century it revived, when Rameses II carried Egyptian arms to the banks of the Orontes, where at Kadesh he met the Hittites in a great battle, in which he claims to have won the victory. The victory was not exploited, however, by the further advance of Egyptian arms. Following his reign a period of Egyptian quiescence set in until the time of Solomon, when Gezer was captured by the Pharaoh and given to Solomon's Egyptian wife as a dowry (1 Kings 9: 16), and the reign of Rehoboam, when Shishak, a Pharaoh of another dynasty, carried his arms through the two kingdoms into which Israel had now split. During the later period of the monarchy Egyptian and Assyrian ambitions involved Israel, and again, when Assyria fell, Egyptian and Babylonian rivalries swept her into their current. Thereafter Egypt exercised no influence on the Jews until the time of Alexander the Great and the Ptolemies.

4. Nearer Neighbours. Of the nearer neighbours of Israel something must be said. The Philistines settled on the coasts of Palestine early in the twelfth century B.C. Where they came from cannot be said with certainty. What is beyond dispute is that they came as the result of the considerable displacements of peoples that accompanied and followed the fall of the Minoan empire, with its centre in Crete. They were a non-Semitic people, and they appear to have been the only people of Palestine who did not practise circumcision.

The immediate neighbours to the south-east have been already mentioned, viz. the Ammonites, the Moabites. and the Edomites. According to the Hebrew traditions these peoples were of a common origin with the Israelites, and the Moabite language, as represented on the Moabite Stone (Plate 15), is scarcely distinguishable from Hebrew. The Ammonites and Moabites are said to be descended from Lot, the nephew of Abraham, while the Edomites are said to be the descendants of Abraham through Jacob's brother Esau. There was constant hostility between these peoples and Israel, however, and during the exile the Jews who remained in the land were subjected to such pressure from the Edomites that ever afterwards the Edomites were regarded with bitter enmity, and the name Edom could be applied to the Romans, when they became their worst enemies.

To the south of Palestine are assigned various tribes that seem to have led a principally nomadic life. These included the Amalekites, who were regarded with the fiercest hostility, and the Midianites, who figure in the story only until the time of Gideon. The Amalekites are not regarded as in any way akin to the Israelites, but the Midianites are traced back to Abraham. They are also associated with the Kenites, some of whom accompanied the Israelites from the days of the wilderness wanderings and seem to have been absorbed into Israel.

When the Israelites entered Palestine, they found a mixed population there, and no less than seven different peoples are named in some of the lists. This mixed population doubtless reflected the complex history of the region from the earliest times. Some scholars believe that the Canaanites entered the land about 3000 B.C., but we have insufficient evidence to decide when they came, or where they came from. The Israelite conquest was not carried through swiftly, and large numbers of the earlier inhabitants remained, to be gradually assimilated with the Israelite tribes.

North of Palestine lay a number of states, few of which figure in the Bible. The Phoenician kingdom, whose chief cities were Tyre and Sidon, was of great importance. By their geographical situation these cities naturally looked to the sea for their livelihood, and they achieved considerable maritime influence in the Mediterranean and founded colonies at a number of places on its shores. Their language was Semitic, and little different from Hebrew. In material culture they were more advanced than the Israelites, and when the Temple was built Tyrian artificers were employed. Later Omri allied himself with Tyre in order to strengthen his position, though Jezebel, in whose marriage with Ahab the alliance was sealed, proved the undoing of Omri's house.

North of Tyre on the coast lay the Phoenician city of Gebal, known to the Greeks as Byblos. According to Joshua 13: 5 it lay within the Promised Land, but it was never actually included in Israelite territory. Modern excavations have brought to light inscriptions written in a script so far undeciphered, which provides evidence that here in the second millennium B.C. experiments were being made to find a more satisfactory method of writing. These experiments seem to have been roughly contemporaneous with the experiments in a simplified cuneiform that were made at Ugarit.

The very old city of Damascus figures frequently in the Bible. It lies in a fertile plain, east of the Anti-Lebanon, and is watered by the Abana. It was the seat of an Aramaean kingdom which was conquered by David, but which soon arose again and in the ninth century B.C. was a constant menace to Israel until weakened by Assyrian attacks. It was finally conquered by Assyria in 732 B.C. In the New Testament it figures only in connexion with the conversion of St. Paul.

Here in the street called Straight (Plate 24), which still exists, Paul was staying when he was visited by Ananias, had his sight restored, and was baptized (Acts 9: 10 ff.).

Lying on the coast opposite Cyprus is the modern *Râs Shamra*, which French excavations have shown to be the ancient Ugarit. This is not mentioned in the Bible, but is known from ancient inscriptions from Egypt and elsewhere, as well as from the Amarna Letters. It was the centre of an important kingdom, and its significance for the student of the Bible lies in the contents of some of the inscriptions in the alphabetic cuneiform that was invented there. Many of these are mythological texts, and as the Ugaritic language is closely related to Phoenician or Canaanite, and a common cultural and religious pattern seems to have extended through Syria and Palestine, they give us a fuller knowledge of the religious ideas of the Canaanites than we have elsewhere. Ugarit itself was destroyed before the Israelite conquest of Palestine, but there is reason to think that fundamentally its religion was common to the whole land, even though the Ugaritic literature may reflect a local variety of that religion. Its pantheon seems to have been shared with the whole land: e.g. the name of the goddess Anath appears in the name of Jeremiah's birthplace, Anathoth; and in the light of its texts much in the Old Testament takes on a clearer light. Its poetic forms are paralleled in the Old Testament, and many of its phrases have their counterpart in the Bible.

5. More Distant Lands. Farther to the east than Babylonia lies Elam, which figures in the story of Genesis 14 and in some of the prophetic oracles. During the period when Babylonia was struggling to secure its independence of Assyria, before the founding of the Neo-Babylonian empire, Elam was allied with Babylon, and its capital, Susa, was captured and sacked by Ashurbanipal. Later, Elam became a part of the Median empire, and then of the Persian, and Susa was the seat of the Persian court for part of the year (Neh. 1: 1).

Media lay north of Elam and east of Assyria. During the last century of the Assyrian empire hordes of invaders from the Caucasus region pressed into Assyria, and their advance was with difficulty stemmed. Some were diverted into Asia Minor and others into Media. Here they became merged with the Medes and contributed their strength to the Median empire, which included Elam and Persia. At the time of the collapse of the Assyrian empire they were allied with the Babylonians, and Nineveh fell to their arms. About half a century later, however, the prince of the little Persian state of Anshan revolted successfully against Media and established the Persian empire, which first swallowed up the Median empire and then spread to Asia Minor to annex the kingdom of Croesus, and finally overcame the Neo-Babylonian empire. Under the son of Cyrus Egypt was added to the Persian domains. Thus the Jews came under the dominion of the Persians, and were subject to Persian religious and cultural influences.

When the Persian empire fell to Alexander the Great, the Jews were brought under Hellenistic rule, and influences emanating from Europe became for the first time a powerful factor in their life. Alexander founded Alexandria, and large numbers of Jews soon settled there. When, after the death of Alexander, his generals carved out kingdoms for themselves from his dominions, the Ptolemies secured Egypt and also Palestine, so that not only did Greek influence touch the Jews of the Diaspora who lived in Egypt, but in Palestine itself the same influence was felt. In the north the Seleucids established their rule in Syria and founded Antioch (Plate 25) to become their capital. From the start they had aspirations to rule Palestine, which was for a century a bone of contention between Ptolemies and Seleucids, until at last the transfer was effected, when Greek influence became even more pressing.

Already, however, Rome was on the horizon, and within a few years of Palestine's coming under Seleucid rule, Rome had humiliated Antiochus III in Asia Minor, and a few years later even more grievously humiliated Antiochus IV in Egypt. Not for another century and more were Roman arms seen in Palestine, however, until Pompey came to Jerusalem. From then on, Palestine became more definitely orientated to the Mediterranean world, as a part of the Roman empire, and in the New Testament there is no longer any looking towards the east. Instead eyes were to the west, and already in the Gospels we find the evidence of the burning desire in some Jewish circles to be delivered from Rome that led ultimately to the disaster of A.D. 70. Yet Roman rule, however harshly the Jews may have felt its yoke, was not an unmixed evil. It gave security through a vast area and good communications, and Jews and Christians were profited thereby.

3

The Identification of Biblical Sites

EVERY user of an Atlas expects to find places marked to indicate their exact position. Yet when different Biblical maps are compared, the same city may be found located in quite different positions. Sometimes a question mark will testify to some uncertainty as to the position, but there is often a real element of doubt even where no question mark is used. In some cases older scholars favoured one identification of a site, while today this has been universally replaced by another. In other cases contemporary scholars are not agreed, and hence recent maps will show marked differences. It should therefore be clear that there are inherent difficulties in the location of many sites, and the reader should understand the nature of these.

Few Biblical towns have been continuously occupied from ancient times until today. Some, after being repeatedly destroyed and rebuilt, were long since permanently abandoned and allowed to fall into ruin to form the tells which are found throughout the ancient Near East. The modern names of these tells sometimes bear an obvious resemblance to the names of Biblical towns which must have been in the neighbourhood. But before we leap to identify them, the evidence needs to be carefully examined. The excavation of a tell may yield clear evidence which puts the matter out of doubt. Thus, excavations at the modern *el-Jîb*, which has long been thought to preserve the name Gibeon, have now definitely confirmed this identification by producing large numbers of jar-handles stamped with the name Gibeon, together with a clay funnel which fits the mouths of some of the jars, thus clearly suggesting that the jars were made to be filled here and exported to other places.

Sometimes the ancient name has been transferred to a neighbouring site. Thus the name Jericho is preserved in the name of the modern village of *Erîkhā*, near which lie the ruins of the Old Testament Jericho at *Tell es-Sulṭân*, and of New Testament Jericho at *Khirbet en-Nitla*. Similarly the modern *Beisân* preserves the name of Beth-shan, whose ruins lie close at hand at *Tell el-Ḥuṣn*, where very important excavations have yielded valuable Egyptian inscriptions.

Not seldom, however, the modern names bear little resemblance to the Biblical names. Thus the ancient Shechem (Plate 9) is today known as *Tell Balâṭah*. Here the Biblical evidence of the position of Shechem points clearly to this spot, and modern excavations have proved it beyond doubt. Similarly modern archaeology has established that *Tell el-Mutesellim* is the ancient Megiddo. Conder suggested the identification with the modern *Mujadda'*, three miles south of Beth-shan, on the ground of the similarity of the names. But the name is less similar than it appears to the English reader, and the association of Megiddo with Taanach provided a serious difficulty. Hence the site of *Tell el-Mutesellim* was more generally favoured, even before excavations settled the question.

The site of the Biblical Mizpah, west of the Jordan, was long uncertain, until excavations at *Tell en-Naṣbeh* made it almost certain that it should be located there. Again, various sites had been suggested for Tirzah, until the excavations of Father de Vaux at *Tell el-Fâr'ah* showed that the history of the site corresponded very closely with the Biblical evidence, and rendered it highly probable, to say the least, that here we have the site of Israel's capital immediately prior to Omri's creation of the city of Samaria. The modern *Tell el-Ḥesī* was long regarded as the Biblical Lachish, until excavations at *Tell ed-Duweir*, which yielded the important Lachish Letters (Plate 18), made it plain that Lachish stood at the latter site.

It will be seen that even where excavations have been carried out, the evidence is often insufficient to establish a location with certainty, though it may attain a high degree of probability. Far more difficult, however, is the case of the many sites where no excavations have taken place. Here the modern names may sometimes offer a *prima facie* identification, but we cannot be sure that there has been a continuous transmission from ancient times until now. Where the Biblical traditions about a place enable us to fix its approximate location, and this accords with the *prima facie* identification, a greater probability may be recognized.

Some ancient extra-Biblical sources of information offer us help, though it is not always so precise as could be desired. The Pharaoh Shishak, who invaded Palestine in the reigns of Rehoboam and Jeroboam I, left an account of his campaign containing a large number of Israelite towns. Their order seemed arbitrary, however, and the account seemed to offer little guidance as to the relative situation of the towns, until Dr. Mazar showed that the first four lines of the text should be read boustrophedon, i.e. one line should be read from left to right and the next from right to left. Certainly identifiable places then fell into line and made it probable that the intervening places lay along the roads joining them, and allowed a consistent itinerary to be followed. On the Moabite Stone (Plate 15) some places mentioned in the Old Testament figure, and similarly on the inscriptions of Assyrian kings. These sources have all to be used with care, but they are not without value.

More valuable is the evidence of Josephus, who in the course of his writings gives a great deal of topographical information. As he lived in Palestine for much of his life and was one of the rebel commanders at the opening of the Jewish War, this is very important evidence for the first century of our era. At a later date, in the fourth century, Eusebius prepared his *Onomasticon*, consisting of a kind of Gazetteer of the Holy Land, giving the identifications of Biblical sites accepted in his day—not necessarily all reliable—and the distances of the lesser known sites from those better known.

By the use of these various sources very different degrees of probability attach to the identifications which are more favoured today. Where several lines of evidence converge, probability is increased, but in the case of many sites we are left with little clear evidence, and new excavations may at any time involve the revision of our location of Biblical places. For the identifications given in the present Atlas, Abel's masterly *Géographie de la Palestine* (Paris, 1938) has been constantly used, and the more recent work of J. Simons, *The Geographical and Topographical Texts of the Old Testament* (Leiden, 1959), has been much consulted. In addition, the various recent Atlases of the Bible have been used. These include the works of P. Lemaire and D. Baldi (Turin, 1954), G. E. Wright and F. V. Filson (revised edition, Philadelphia and London, 1956), L. H. Grollenberg (Edinburgh, 1956), and E. G. Kraeling (New York, 1956). The little work of M. du Buit, *Géographie de la Terre Sainte* (Paris, 1958), has also been consulted, as have many other works which have been drawn on for special points.

Plate 1

Above: Taskwork in Egypt
Below: The Road to Sinai

Plate 2

Plate 3

Mount Sinai (*Jebel Mûsā*)

Plate 4

Above: The Arnon Gorge
Below: The Dead Sea and the Promised Land (from Mt. Nebo)

Plate 5

Plate (

The River Jordan

Plate 7

Above: Jerusalem from the air (from the south-west)
Below: Jerusalem showing the " Dome of the Rock " (the temple site)

Plate 8

Plate

Above: Shechem, showing Gerizim (*left*) and Ebal (*right*)
Below: Samaria

Plate I

Plate 11

Above: The Kidron Valley
Below: Jerusalem from the air (from the east)

Plate 12

Plate I

Above: The Lebanon (looking over Ba'albek)
Below: The Sea of Galilee (with Hermon in the distance)

Plate

—4—

Archaeology and Biblical Study

IN the previous chapter the contribution of archaeology to the determination of some Biblical sites has been briefly indicated. It is not to be supposed, however, that this is the principal contribution of archaeology to the study of the Bible. In countless ways it has thrown light on the study of the sacred text, and today it is of the first importance to the Biblical student to take account of all the material it provides. Clearly no full account of its finds and of their significance can be given here, where all that is possible is to illustrate simply the variety of ways in which it helps us.

For more than a century Egyptian and Mesopotamian archaeology has been freely drawn on by writers on the Old Testament. Ever since the great monuments of Egypt have been deciphered they have been studied to see how the story of the Bible can be related to the history which they unfold. Similarly, the Babylonian and Assyrian texts have been used as they became available. The Assyrian kings tell in their inscriptions of their campaigns, and from them we can learn much of the international background of Israel's history. Here we learn of the coalition of Syrian and Palestinian princes that opposed Shalmaneser III at the battle of Ḳarḳar in 853 B.C., and since there were contingents from Israel, including substantial contingents of chariots, light is shed on the peace that Ahab made with Benhadad before that battle, after he had defeated the army of the king of Damascus in the field (1 Kings 20: 34). To the reader of the Bible, which does not mention the battle of Ḳarḳar, the behaviour of Ahab seems quixotic, but it is clear that it was under a larger menace that Samaria and Damascus for a short time drew together. Jehu's payment of tribute to the Assyrian monarch (Plate 17), and Sennacherib's own account (Plate 16) of the campaign of 701 B.C. (which forms the background of the Biblical story of part of the reign of Hezekiah), have long been known to us, and a great deal else besides.

Much new material has come to light during the last forty years. A part of the Babylonian Chronicle gave us more exact knowledge of the events that preceded and followed the fall of Nineveh than we had before, and enabled us to date that fall with precision. It also made it clear that when Josiah opposed Pharaoh Neco and lost his life (2 Kings 23: 29), he was not pathetically loyal to his Assyrian overlord, as had been supposed, but was harassing the ally of Assyria in a bid for independence. Further parts of the Chronicle have quite recently come to light, enabling us to trace the events that followed the downfall of the Assyrian kingdom. The Egyptian forces were defeated at the battle of Carchemish and beat a hasty retreat to Egypt, but Egypt was not at once eliminated as a force to be reckoned with, as we had supposed. In 601 B.C. a further fierce engagement was fought in the south of Palestine.

Just before the Second World War opened, some tablets from Babylon were published, and on these are recorded the rations allowed to Jehoiachin and his sons. Some scholars had supposed that because Jeremiah had prophesied "Write this man down as childless" (Jer. 22: 30), Jehoiachin had no children, and that the Chronicler, who gives the names of seven of his sons (1 Chron. 3: 17 f.), was not to be relied on, and the New Testament genealogy of our Lord, which included

Jehoiachin amongst His ancestors (Matt. 1: 12), was incorrect.

From Mari, where many campaigns have been undertaken, vast numbers of texts have come, and these in many ways serve the student of the Bible. From them we learn that Ḫammurabi of Babylon was contemporary with Zimri-lim of Mari, who can be dated in the eighteenth century B.C. This has brought down the date of Ḫammurabi much later than had been supposed. It was once common to equate Amraphel of Genesis 14: 2 with Ḫammurabi, and thus to make Abraham contemporary with that monarch. It is now clear that either Abraham must be brought down much later than the Biblical chronology suggests, or the equivalence of the names must be given up, in which case we are left without any link with Ḫammurabi for the dating of Abraham.

From Mari also we learn that the phenomenon of prophecy was found there. The Egyptian text of Wenamon already gave us evidence of prophecy at Byblos in the eleventh century B.C., and it had long been recognized that this was a phenomenon of more than Israelite significance. Indeed, the Old Testament testifies to the existence of prophets of Baal in the time of Elijah. But the non-Israelite existence of such prophecy is now carried back much earlier and more widely afield. This does not materially affect our estimate of prophecy in Israel. It was already freely recognized that it was not unique in its origin, but that its uniqueness lay in what it became in the greater prophetic figures of the Old Testament.

Again, the Code of Ḫammurabi has been known since the beginning of the present century. Its laws have been compared with the laws of the Pentateuch, and it has been recognized that Israelite law had behind it a wider background of ancient Near Eastern law. Today we have a much fuller knowledge of that background. Ḫammurabi's Code was not a new creation, for older codes have now come to light, such as those of Ur-nammu, Lipit-Ishtar, and Eshnunna. Moreover, from Nuzu many legal texts have come to light which give us valuable knowledge of the law and custom of that city—roughly in the age of the patriarchs. From these light has been shed on customs which figure in the patriarchal narratives. In Nuzu it was common for a childless man to adopt a son, sometimes a slave, as Abraham adopted Eliezer (Gen. 15: 2). Yet in the adoption deeds it is specified that if the adopter subsequently begot a son, the adopted son would yield precedence to him (cf. Gen. 15: 4). Again, it is laid down in marriage contracts at Nuzu that if a wife proved childless, she should be under obligation to provide her husband with a slave wife to bear children in her stead, precisely as happened in the case of Abraham and Jacob. We read of the sale of a birthright, as we do in the Old Testament (Gen. 25: 29 ff.). Rachel's theft of her father's teraphim (Gen. 31: 32) is seen in a new light when we learn from Nuzu that the possession of such images carried with it the title to the inheritance of property.

In an earlier chapter mention has been made of the important Ugaritic texts found at *Râs Shamra*, and of their many-sided value to the Biblical student, and they must be left without further mention here.

For three-quarters of a century we have had knowledge of the Amarna Letters, discovered in Egypt on the site of the heretic Pharaoh Akhenaton's ephemeral capital, Akhetaton, with the light they throw on conditions in Palestine in the fourteenth century B.C. They tell of trouble caused by people who are named in some of the texts by the ideogram SA-GAZ and in others called Ḫabiru, and these have been identified by many writers with the Biblical Hebrews—though the equation of the names is less simple than it may appear to the English reader. From Egyptian texts we knew of 'Aperu in Egypt, whose identity with the Ḫabiru was affirmed by some and denied by others. Now from Ugarit we have secure evidence of the equation of these two names, while from Nuzu we have evidence of numbers of Ḫabiru in that city, many of whom voluntarily accepted the status of slaves. The whole question of the Ḫabiru has become much more complicated, and they were certainly a far more widespread people than the Israelites who came out of Egypt under Moses. Whether the term is of ethnic significance or whether it denoted a social class is not agreed.

Early in the present century some Aramaic texts from Elephantine in Egypt, an island opposite Assuan, were published. These told us of a Jewish military colony on the island in the fifth century B.C. They had their own temple of Yahu, who is to be identified with the Yahweh of the Old Testament. Towards the end of the century their temple was destroyed by their Egyptian neighbours, and the colonists sought the help of Samaria and Jerusalem in an attempt to have the rebuilding of the temple authorized by the Persian authorities. Since they appealed to Delaiah and Shelemiah, the sons of Sanballat, the governor of Samaria, it is probable that Sanballat was old and his sons administered the land in his name. Hence the age of Nehemiah, whose work fell in the time when Sanballat himself exercised control, must have belonged to the reign of Artaxerxes I. On the other hand, the appeal to Jerusalem was sent to the High Priest Johanan, who was contemporary with Ezra, whereas Nehemiah was contemporary with Johanan's grandfather Eliashib. It therefore becomes probable that Johanan continued to be High Priest into the reign of Artaxerxes II, and that Ezra's mission fell in that king's reign.

These few illustrations must suffice to show the various ways in which finds from sites outside Palestine throw light on the Bible. They rarely give us direct confirmation of any Biblical event, and it is going beyond the evidence to say they " prove " the accuracy of the Bible, as is sometimes done. Few Biblical characters find specific mention in any text. Nevertheless, they are of the greatest value. They enable us to place the history of Israel in the period of the monarchy in the wider setting of world history, while for the period of the patriarchs they show that the customs reflected in the traditions are the true customs of the period.

Coming to Palestinian archaeology, we are immediately faced with the paucity of texts which have come to light, save from one neighbourhood, which will be mentioned below. From Gezer we have a small tablet, perhaps from the tenth century B.C., but it contains nothing more than the months of the year defined according to the agricultural operations proper to them. From Dibon we have the already mentioned Moabite Stone (Plate 15), on which Mesha, the king of Moab, who is mentioned in 2 Kings 3: 4, records the story of his successful revolt from Israel. He tells us—what we do not learn from the Bible—that Moab had been subject to Israel for forty years, and also that there was a temple of Yahweh at Nebo. The Siloam inscription, inscribed on the living rock in the tunnel that carried water to the pool of Siloam, tells of the construction of the tunnel, and probably dates from the time of Hezekiah. The

Bible tells us of Hezekiah's measures for the water supply of Jerusalem (2 Kings 20: 20), and it is almost certain that the reference is to the construction of this tunnel.

All of these texts have long been known. Twenty-five years ago, when *Tell ed-Duweir* was excavated, the Lachish Letters (Plate 18) were brought to light. These were inscribed on pieces of broken pottery in the reign of Zedekiah, shortly before the fall of Jerusalem. They contain military messages, and bring little increase of our knowledge of historical events, but introduce us to the atmosphere of tension that prevailed in the sorely beset garrison. Their language and style have many points of contact with the book of Jeremiah, and here we read of a prophet who " weakened the hands " of the people, precisely as Jeremiah himself was accused of doing (Jer. 38: 4). Some have thought the prophet was indeed Jeremiah himself, but as only the termination of the name has survived, this cannot be established.

From other sites jar-handles and seals have been found —amongst the latter being the seal of Shemaʿ, the servant of Jeroboam, found in Megiddo, and the seal of Jaazaniah, perhaps the person mentioned in 2 Kings 25: 23, found at Mizpah. Samaria has yielded a number of ostraca—inscribed pieces of pottery, like the Lachish Letters—apparently invoices for the delivery of jars of wine and oil to the royal household.

Of greater importance than these finds are the excavations which have yielded no written texts, or no more than the occasional find of a seal. For the modern archaeological technique enables the excavator to trace the history of a site, on which sometimes several successive cities stood. Every level is marked by broken bits of pottery, and by these the dates of the various levels can be determined. Mention has been made above of the Danish excavations at Shiloh, which established the destruction of the city in the middle of the eleventh century B.C., and made it probable that it was destroyed by the Philistines after the death of Eli. The excavation of a number of sites has shown that they suffered a major disaster towards the end of the thirteenth century B.C., and while there is nothing to connect this destruction with the incoming Israelites, it is probable that they were so connected, since some of these places are mentioned in the Bible as taken by Israel. Two places provide special problems of their own, and it is not easy to integrate the archaeological and the Biblical evidence. These are Ai and Jericho. Here it is possible that older destructions which were remembered in tradition were associated with Joshua; but it is impossible to discuss the complexities of these problems here.

Not only in these cases but also in others it frequently happens that archaeology complicates our problem rather than simplifies it. The outstanding example of this is the question of the Exodus, where Biblical and non-Biblical evidence from a wide variety of places, including excavations at Biblical sites and evidence from Egypt, Mesopotamia, and Ugarit, renders the integration of all into a single self-consistent account quite impossible.

Of all the written finds from Palestine the Dead Sea Scrolls are by far the most important and the most unexpected. The first scrolls were found by a Bedouin boy, and from the cave in which they were found seven manuscripts and two jars were taken. Later, when archaeologists examined the cave, they found buried beneath accumulations of dirt broken fragments of similar jars and fragments of many manuscripts, including fragments of some of the actual manuscripts already carried away. From other caves in the neighbourhood fragments of large numbers of manuscripts were discovered, and in the eleventh cave some further major manuscripts, comparable with those in the first cave, were found. Meanwhile the excavation of a ruined site in the neighbourhood yielded evidence that this was the centre used by the people who once owned the manuscripts, and made it probable that many of them were actually copied here. The centre seems to have come into existence in the second century B.C., and to have been destroyed by the Romans in A.D. 68. All the evidence goes to show that the people from whom the Scrolls came were the sect that became known in the first century of our era as the Essenes. Some of their texts were copies of Biblical manuscripts, and while many of them exist now only in fragments, they are of real value for the textual criticism of the Bible. Amongst the manuscripts from the first cave, there is one complete manuscript of the book of Isaiah, and also a substantial though incomplete manuscript of the same book. Other manuscripts contain texts which reflect the history, ideas, and practices of the sect, and these are of high importance for the study of the intertestamental period, and particularly of currents in the Judaism of the beginning of the Christian era. There are many links of word and thought with passages of the New Testament, though there are even more important differences between the sect and the early Church. It can scarcely be doubted that this sect belonged to the world in which Jesus exercised His ministry. In some things it may well have influenced the early Church, while in others sayings of our Lord and passages in the New Testament may have been directed against them. In any case, the importance of the Scrolls is very high indeed, though the historical allusions they contain are in most cases so cryptic that they cannot be used with security for the history of the period.

All of the finds so far mentioned were made in the neighbourhood of *Qumrân*. Some miles farther south, at *Murabba'at*, other finds have been made. These include a number of fragments of Biblical books, but no sectarian texts which can be connected with the Qumrân sect. They include two letters written by Bar Cochba, who led the revolt of the Jews in A.D. 132. These letters can therefore be securely dated, and they now set a standard for the study of the palaeography of the Qumrân Scrolls which was wanting before. They show that the Qumrân Scrolls are older than these letters, and so confirm the view that the Qumrân Scrolls were deposited in the caves earlier than the time of Bar Cochba.

In one of the Qumrân caves an inscribed copper scroll, containing an inventory of treasure, was found. There is nothing to show that this copper scroll was prepared in the Qumrân centre, and as it contains a reference to another copy deposited elsewhere, it may well have been itself prepared elsewhere and have been deposited in the cave for additional security as a guarantee against the loss of the other copy. Of the theories about this treasure the most probable is that it was an inventory of Temple treasure, which was removed and hidden while it was still possible, before the destruction of the Temple. While it is impossible to discuss the Dead Sea Scrolls at length here, no account of Biblical archaeology, however brief, could leave them without mention.

From this short survey, which aims to be illustrative only, the reader will see that archaeology is of very varied use to the student of the Bible. It yields historical materials and fills in the background of our knowledge at many points, it sheds light on the culture and everyday life of the people of days long past, and it gives us fuller knowledge of the religious environment in which Israel lived as well as of the practice and ideas of a Jewish sect that is unmentioned in the New Testament, but that is known to us from writers of the first century of our era.

—5—

Wandering and Settlement

THE Bible opens with the stories of Creation and of the Garden of Eden. No Atlas of the Bible can show the location of Eden, though many authors have discussed where the writer of the story conceived of it as lying. It is impossible to regard the story as literal history, though this does not mean that it is to be dismissed as childish mythology. A profound meaning of enduring value penetrates the whole story, and attention to its form and the aetiological details which may be found in it without grasping the essential message it contains is as unperceptive as the minute examination of a nutshell by one who carelessly threw away the kernel. Its purpose is to say that man was created by God for His own obedience, and that in that obedience alone man's true well-being was to be found, but that man was created free to obey or to disobey and that he chose to disobey. By this disobedience he not only brought on himself exclusion from God's presence and the loss of his own well-being; he excluded himself. Before he was turned out of the Garden of Eden he hid himself from the presence of God. For the essential character of sin is that it isolates man from God and curses the sinner. The Bible begins not with science or with history but with religion.

On this and other stories in the early chapters of the Bible we cannot linger here. It is well known that the stories of Creation and the Flood are related to Babylonian stories, and that of the building of the tower of Babel clearly relates to the city of Babylon and the *ziggurat* or temple of Marduk which was found there.

Since the Bible tells how the first ancestor of the Israelite people once lived in the Babylonian city of Ur, it is not surprising that there should be this link with Babylonian stories of human origins. What has equally to be noted is the transformation of the stories in their Biblical form. All the crude polytheism of the Babylonian stories is gone, and a spiritual message pervades the whole. Once more the meaning, rather than the details of the form, should have the focus of attention.

It is only when we come to Abraham that we begin to touch history, and even here not very securely. Abraham cannot be set firmly in the framework of world history, and nothing recorded about him can be related to known events. It has been said above that if the equation of Amraphel with Ḫammurabi of Babylon is maintained, then Abraham must be placed in the eighteenth or seventeenth century B.C. and the Biblical chronology must be abandoned. In fact both the equation and the chronology raise difficulties. Not a few scholars assign Abraham to the nineteenth century B.C. Of the events narrated in Genesis 14 we have no record elsewhere, and the kings whose names figure in the story cannot be identified with security. It is widely held today that this chapter is older than the main sources of the Pentateuch, and that it embodies an ancient tradition.

That there is historical substance in the traditions about Abraham seems more probable today than it once did. It has already been said that the customs reflected in the patriarchal stories are now known to have been truly the customs of the second millennium B.C., and there is a presumption that stories which have preserved the contemporary colour may have preserved genuine historical memories. If the patriarchs were no more than the creations of later minds, it would be hard to understand why Abraham should be depicted as a man of such exalted character, Isaac a rather colourless person, and Jacob, the immediate ancestor of the Israelite tribes, a man of so much meaner a character.

Abraham is said to have lived originally in Ur, and to have left it for Haran with his father (Gen. 11: 31). Ur was an ancient Sumerian city, which has been excavated in modern times and has yielded evidences of a thick layer of deposit which must have been caused by flood. Before we conclude that this confirms the Biblical Flood story, however, we must remember that in neighbouring towns similar deposits left at different periods have been found, and that in one town there is evidence that the Babylonian Flood story was known before such a deposit was left. That there is verisimilitude in the story of a migration from Ur to Haran is indicated by the fact that Ur was the greatest centre of the worship of the Moon god, Sin, and that Haran in Upper Mesopotamia, on the banks of the Habor, was also a notable centre of the worship of the same deity. From Haran Abraham set out with his nephew Lot for Canaan, where he came into association with a number of places, including Shechem, Hebron, Jerusalem, and Gerar. He is also said to have journeyed into Egypt, where his wife was brought for a time into the Pharaoh's palace. His nephew settled in Sodom, one of the Cities of the Plain whose destruction through some natural disaster was remembered for many centuries, but whose precise location can no longer be determined.

Abraham retained his connexion with his own family, and when he sought a wife for his son Isaac, he sent to Aram-naharaim to secure a woman of his own kindred (Gen. 24). Like his father, Isaac moved about from place to place, and is said to have gone to Gerar at one time. But here there is a clear anachronism in the story, since Gerar is said to have been the seat of the king of the Philistines. On any chronology Isaac must be dated before the Philistine immigration.

In the next generation Jacob returns to his kindred in Mesopotamia, where he not only finds his wives but spends many years before returning to the land of Canaan. He is brought into association with the shrine of Bethel, which is legitimated for his descendants by the theophany granted to him there (Gen. 28: 10 ff.), with Penuel, where he wrestles with the angelic visitor (Gen. 32: 22 ff.), and with Hebron, from which he sends Joseph to visit his brothers in Shechem (Gen. 37: 14), though when Joseph arrives there he finds they have moved to Dothan. Soon the scene shifts to Egypt, whither Joseph is carried as a slave, to rise later to high office in the land, to which in course of time his brothers and his father come, to settle in the land of Goshen and to remain for the long years that ended in the Oppression.

That there is some historical kernel in all this cannot reasonably be doubted. Nevertheless, it cannot be treated as modern scientific history, and whoever tries seriously to relate it and the subsequent events to known history will quickly become aware of the problems it raises. The Biblical chronology would place Abraham in the twenty-first century B.C., the migration of Jacob to Egypt in the nineteenth century, and the Exodus in the middle of the fifteenth century. Yet though the length of the sojourn in Egypt is stated in Exodus 12: 40 to have been 430 years, the genealogies preserved in the Bible show that normally four generations covered the period. Further, no reader would suppose that between Exodus 1: 6 and 8 lay a period of more than 200 years.

It is therefore likely that the period spent in Egypt was much shorter than 430 years.

When Jacob went into Egypt, he and his family were settled in Goshen (Gen. 47: 6), where they still remained at the time of the Exodus (Exod. 8: 22). During the Oppression they were set to work on store cities in this district, and their names are given as Pithom and Raamses (Exod. 1: 11). The latter is to be identified with Pi-Ramesse, a city which was once known as Avaris, and later as Tanis or Zoan. As later Israelite memories con-nect the Exodus story with Zoan (Ps. 78: 12, 43), this brings a confirming tradition. Avaris was once the capital of the Asiatic conquerors of Egypt known as the Hyksos, who ruled the land from 1720 to 1580 B.C. It then sank into insignificance until the end of the fourteenth century, when it was rebuilt by Rameses II and named after him. Later its name was changed to Tanis.

There are two main theories of the date of the Exodus. The one places it in the middle of the fifteenth century B.C., and identifies the Israelites under Joshua with the enemies referred to in the Amarna Letters, but this requires the dismissal of the references to Raamses or Tanis, and involves other difficulties which will appear below. The other places the Exodus in the thirteenth century B.C., either during the reign of Rameses II or at the beginning of the reign of his successor, Merneptah. The thirteenth-century dating is the more widely favoured, and is almost certainly to be preferred.

If this date is accepted and the 430 years of the sojourn in Egypt are retained, then the entry into Egypt would fall in the Hyksos period, and the Egyptian court would have been in the same city (Avaris or Pi-Ramesse) at the time of the entry and at the Exodus. But the Biblical account implies that the family of Jacob was settled far from the court, while at the time of the Oppression they were close by the court, so that Pharaoh's daughter lived within walking distance of their homes (Exod. 2: 5). Further, the Pharaoh whom Joseph served gave Joseph the daughter of the priest of On to wife (Gen. 41: 45). This would have been no honour in the Hyksos period, for the Hyksos did not favour the Sun god, whose principal seat was at On.

If, however, the period of the sojourn is shortened to four generations, the entry into Egypt would fall in the thirteenth century. Joseph's administration would then lie in the reign of Akhenaton, who exalted the Sun god to be the sole god whose worship was permitted in Egypt. In this reign Joseph's marriage to the daughter of the priest of On would be a very high honour. Joseph's power in Egypt would be exercised in the Amarna age, and the non-interference of Egypt in Palestine may have owed something to him. There is, indeed, a good deal of evidence to suggest that not all the Israelite tribes went into Egypt, and the SA-GAZ or Ḫabiru of the Amarna Letters were perhaps groups akin to the Israelites in Egypt, from whom those who entered Egypt had broken off. Such a view would explain why the tribes that did not go into Egypt and those that entered the land under Joshua recognized that they were of a common stock.

That the main wave of the Israelite attack on Canaan took place towards the end of the thirteenth century B.C. is borne out by excavations at a number of sites, which provide evidence of the destruction of many towns and a lowering of the cultural level such as might be expected from this incursion. It is impossible here to discuss all the highly complex problems which surround this whole question, and all that can be done is to indicate the lines of their most probable solution. Thi solution recognizes a very substantial historical kerne in the Biblical traditions.

Some scholars despair of the recovery of any histor from the Biblical accounts, and even Moses, who i said to have led the Israelites out of Egypt, is treatec as a shadowy figure of whom we can know little tha is reliable. But again there seems no reason to doub the main outlines of the story. That Moses was borr and brought up in Egypt and in manhood fled to th wilderness is wholly credible, and his later return tc Egypt to lead out the Israelite tribes would be withou explanation if he had had no earlier connexion wit them. When he did return, we are told that the Israelite had not hitherto worshipped God under the name Yahweh. It has long been believed that Yahweh wa the God whose priest Jethro, the father-in-law of Moses was. But the name of Moses' mother, Jochebed, seem to be compounded of the name of this God. Tha Kenite elements were intermingled with the incomin Israelites, and especially with the tribe of Judah, is made clear in the Bible, and Judah is generally believed tc have been one of the tribes that did not share in th sojourn in Egypt. It is therefore possible that th mother of Moses had some Kenite blood in her, derivec from a marriage that antedated the entry of Jacob an his family into Egypt, and this may explain the fligh of Moses to a Kenite family when he was forced to fle from Egypt. Just as Jacob fled to his mother's kindred so may Moses have done, to return later in the name of the Kenite God to the Israelites whom he led out The character of the religion established by Moses wa lifted to a new level, and was born of the experience through which Moses and his people passed.

No reasonable motive for the creation of the story that the Israelites were once slaves in Egypt can be suggested, unless it was based on fact. The deliverance is not attributed to the prowess of Moses or the people, and such prowess would not be suppressed in tradition if it had been shown in fact. Again, the deliverance would not have been attributed to a God whose name was hitherto unknown to the Israelites as the name of their God, if Moses had not come in the name of such a God. Moses led the people to the sacred mount of Yahweh, where they pledged themselves to this God in the Covenant, in response to the deliverance by which He had brought them out of Egypt. All of this adequately explains why the religion of Israel became a religion of covenant, voluntarily entered into by a people in gratitude for the saving acts of a God who had compassion on them in their helplessness. The fundamental character of the religion of the Old Testament derives from these experiences, and not from the Kenites.

The traditional site of the sacred mountain is *Jebel Mûsa* (Plate 3), in the peninsula of Sinai. This is challenged by many modern scholars, and alternative sites have been proposed. Moreover, the account of the wandering in the wilderness is by no means easy to set out in a single consistent story, and various theories of the route of the Exodus have been advanced. Thirty-eight of the forty years seem to have been spent in the neighbourhood of Kadesh-barnea, and this would reduce the period of the actual wandering to two years. It is perhaps possible that two traditions have been combined, the one dealing with the time preceding the entry into the land before the descent into Egypt (i.e. of the ancestors of all the tribes), and the other dealing with the time preceding the entry into Canaan of the tribes led by Moses. On Maps 6–7 one theory of the route of the Exodus is represented. According to this, Kadesh is reached after a long journey to the south of the Sinai peninsula (Plate 2), and Deuteronomy 1: 2 says that the journey from Sinai to Kadesh required eleven days. But in Exodus 15: 22 ff. we read that after crossing the Red Sea the people journeyed for three days to Marah, where Moses sweetened bitter waters, and where God gave them statutes and ordinances and there tested them. Since Massah means "testing", the reference would seem to be to Massah, which in Exodus 17: 7 is identified with Meribah, while Meribah is located at Kadesh in Numbers 20: 13. There are therefore traces of a tradition that brought the Israelites to Kadesh three days after crossing the Red Sea, and this would link with the request to Pharaoh to allow them to journey three days into the wilderness to sacrifice to Yahweh (Exod. 5: 3). Once more, therefore, there are complex problems which cannot be examined in the space at our disposal here.

By whatever route they travelled, the tribes led out by Moses, who seem to have been principally the Joseph tribes, but certainly with some Levite elements, came to Mount Nebo, from the top of which the land west of the Jordan could be viewed (Plate 5), where Moses died, and from here Joshua led them over the Jordan to Gilgal. It has been said above that special problems attach to the story of the fall of Jericho, which may have been of little importance in the time of Joshua. Some scholars, including Albright, have thought that the story of its fall is an older story, which has become attached to the name of Joshua. Further problems surround the fall of Ai, to which Joshua is said to have gone next. Excavation has established that this town lay in ruins throughout most of the second millennium B.C. Here it is possible once more that an older tradition has been transferred to the name of Joshua, or alternatively that an attack on the neighbouring Bethel by Joshua has been transferred to Ai. Other possibilities have been suggested. There seems no reason to doubt that Joshua advanced to this neighbourhood, or that the people of Gibeon were so alarmed that they sought by a ruse to protect themselves by an alliance with Joshua. This in turn led to an attack on Gibeon by a coalition of Palestinian cities, from which Joshua delivered them by a great victory at the battle of Aijalon (Joshua 10).

The book of Joshua gives the impression that the entire land was conquered by the united armies of Israel, after which the land was divided out among the tribes. Yet the opening chapter of the book of Judges represents the conquest as needing still to be achieved after the death of Joshua, and as being then undertaken by the tribes acting separately or in small groups. It is probable that this is the more historical account, especially if the view noted above, that not all the tribes entered in a single body, is correct. The chapters in the second half of the book of Joshua are of very high interest and value, however. They give us much geographical information we do not find elsewhere in the Bible, though it is improbable that they represent the tribal holdings immediately after the entry into Canaan.

6

The Rise and Fall of the Monarchy

IN the book of Judges we have a collection of tribal traditions of the highest value. The earliest of the Judges, Othniel, was a southern leader, and if, as seems probable, he belonged to a group that did not go down into Egypt to be led out by Moses, his exploit may belong to the period before the entry under Joshua. The stories of the Judges are placed in a chronological framework, and the Judges are presented as successive national leaders. They were more probably local leaders, and the contents of the traditions are more valuable than the framework.

Six of the Judges are mere names, and we know nothing of their achievements. Of the other six we have stories preserved. Only one led his people against the Canaanites. The others fought the battles of Israelites and Canaanites alike against external enemies. The deliverance from the Canaanites was achieved by Deborah and Barak in a victory which overthrew the power of Sisera of Harosheth, who was increasing his power over Israelites north and south of the Valley of Jezreel. The victory was commemorated in the magnificent Song of Deborah (Judges 5). It was won against a foe far better equipped than the Israelites, and like the deliverance at the Red Sea it was won with the help of natural forces. A sudden storm reduced the plain to a morass, and immobilized the chariots of Sisera. The significance of this victory lay in that it was won by a larger confederacy of Israelite tribes than was led by any other of the Judges, and in that it brought together in a common enterprise the tribes on both sides of the Valley of Jezreel.

The last Judge mentioned in the book of Judges, Samson, brings us to the beginnings of the conflict with the Philistines. Already the sea people who had settled on the southern shores were moving up the coast, and it was probably due to their pressure that the Danites migrated to the north of the land and seized Laish, which they renamed Dan, where they established a sanctuary with the grandson of Moses as their priest (Judges 18). Samson was a Danite who, by personal feats rather than by tribal leadership, sought to check and harry the Philistines.

Throughout the period of the Judges there was little lasting cohesion amongst the Israelite tribes, and we find frequent evidences of intermarriage and fusion between Israelites and their neighbours. Moral and social conditions were often deplorable, and there was a decline from the standards set by Moses due to the influence of Canaanite religious practice and worship at the local shrines. In times of national crisis it was recognized that Yahweh was not Baal and there was a revival of the national faith, but at other times Yahweh was worshipped under the name of Baal and with the Baalite rites. Once an attempt was made to establish a monarchy (Judges 9), but this proved abortive. It was made by Abimelech, the half-Canaanite son of Gideon, one of the Judges, and it was made in reliance on Canaanite rather than Israelite support. The Judges were in reality charismatic leaders, who owed their position to their qualities of personality, and whose leadership was gradually surrendered when the crisis in which they figured was past.

From the prominence of sanctuaries in the story it

has been conjectured that the Israelite tribes at this time were linked together in groups bound by a common oath to help one another, after the pattern of the Greek amphictyonies. That they recognized moral obligations to one another, though they were not always faithful to them, seems clear, and it is likely that these obligations were felt to rest on the recognition that they were of a common stock and worshipped the same God.

The exploits of Samson did little to stem the advance of the Philistines, and it was under their menace that the monarchy was established in Israel. Eli, the priest of Shiloh and custodian of the sacred symbol known as the Ark, which had come down from the time of Moses, is represented as a Judge, though he is unmentioned in the book of Judges and gave no leadership in any national crisis comparable with that of the other Judges. In his days the Philistines won a great victory over the Israelites at Aphek and captured the Ark, which had been taken on to the field of battle (1 Sam. 4). Shiloh and its shrine were destroyed, and though the Ark was soon returned by the Philistines, when it was found that a plague accompanied it wherever it went, it was kept in obscurity at Kiriath-jearim for many years. The Philistines now established their control over the central highlands, and the fortunes of Israel sank to a low ebb. They rose once more when a prophet, Samuel, supported by bands of prophets who roused patriotic fervour in the name of the national God, encouraged the Benjamite Saul to take the lead against his people's foes (1 Sam. 10: 1 ff.).

An Ammonite attack on Jabesh-gilead gave Saul his opening. Between his tribe and Jabesh-gilead there was an ancient bond through intermarriage (Judges 21: 14), and when the people of Jabesh-gilead appealed to them for help, Saul summoned the Israelite tribes west of the Jordan to follow him to the relief of Jabesh-gilead, and quickly defeated the Ammonites. This action was not directed against the Philistines, and there was no reason why they should interfere. But the new confidence which was born in Israel, and the recognition of Saul's gifts of leadership, soon led to a blow against the Philistines which dislodged them from the centre of the land, and they were ignominiously defeated at the battle of Michmash. But the Philistine menace was not ended, as menaces had been ended before, by a single victory. Indeed it was to persist for long, and it was the recognition of the need for more continuous leadership which led Samuel to establish Saul as king. Throughout his reign Saul had to face new attacks, but the measure of his success is seen in the fact that while he lived the Philistines did not again establish their control in the heart of the land. At the battle of Ephes-dammim, when Goliath was slain, they were trying to press up the defiles into Judah, and at the end of Saul's reign they went up the coast and into the Valley of Jezreel, all of which they still controlled, to make an attack on the central highlands from the north. Here Saul was slain on the field of Gilboa, and for the time being his work was undone.

Saul's qualities of leadership were marred by an instability of character, and by a jealousy of the youthful David which became an obsession. David was outlawed, and to protect himself he became a dependant of one of the Philistine rulers. Then, on the death of Saul, David's own tribe of Judah made him their king, while Saul's surviving son, Ishbaal (or Ishbosheth), retired east of the Jordan, beyond Philistine influence, and there claimed the succession to his father's throne.

Once more the Philistines watched without concern the conflict between David and Ishbaal. They could scarcely wish their dependant to become too powerful, and for Israelites to waste their strength on one another suited them well. But when Ishbaal was assassinated (2 Sam. 4: 5 ff.) and David was acclaimed king of all Israel, they awoke too late to the situation.

David now turned his arms against Jerusalem, a Jebusite city which had not yet been taken by Israel. Probably it had obstructed David in his conflict with Ishbaal, as we should expect it to obstruct a dependant of the Philistines, who were dreaded by the Canaanites no less than by the Israelites. By a clever ruse David soon entered the city (2 Sam. 5: 6 ff.), whose strength of position had given its inhabitants the belief that it was impregnable. He seems to have treated the people of Jerusalem with clemency, and shortly afterwards made it his capital city, and attached Israelite sentiment to it by bringing the Ark into it. As the Ark had long lain in neglect, the northern tribe of Ephraim, which had formerly had the custody of this sacred symbol, would have reason to be pleased and would be given a link with Jerusalem, while in the person of David the tribe of Judah had a link. More important, David in this way gave a new religious foundation to his rule. The bond which united his people was religious, and that religion was declared to be the religion which had been established by Moses.

Further conquests soon followed. The Philistines now attacked their quondam dependant, only to be defeated and reduced to obedience to him. The neighbouring peoples to south, east, and north were reduced in succession, and a larger kingdom than that ever again achieved in the history of Israel was established. The great empires of Egypt and Mesopotamia were without influence in Palestine at this time, and the tribes of Israel had an opportunity which their unity under David enabled them to exploit. Yet the seeds of disunity appeared during the reign of David, and he had twice to face rebellion, once under the leadership of his own son, Absalom. Both were successfully overcome, largely owing to the ruthless efficiency of Joab, David's commander-in-chief. At the end of David's reign there were succession troubles, out of which Solomon emerged as king, and Adonijah, though temporarily spared, was marked down for destruction when opportunity should offer.

Solomon's reign was marked by a splendour which fascinated later generations. It was mainly a time of peace and hence resources were not consumed by war as in the time of David. The subject peoples paid their dues into Solomon's exchequer, and heavy economic burdens were laid upon his own people. Trade could pass freely through his kingdom, and its tolls were poured into his treasury. In addition, Solomon exploited the copper mines in the neighbourhood of Ezion-geber, from which port his ships sailed on the state-trading enterprises in which he engaged. Yet despite his wealth his extravagances exceeded it, and he was forced to cede territory in settlement of his debts (1 Kings 9: 11). Moreover, the burdens he placed on his people, and especially the burden of forced labour, aroused intense discontent, and at his door, rather than at his son's, lay the responsibility for the division of the kingdom.

For his building enterprises, and especially for the building of the Temple, Solomon relied on the skill of foreign artificers. Built to be a royal sanctuary and attached to the palace, it exceeded in magnificence any sanctuary in the land. Older sanctuaries had the prestige of their associations, which they long retained, but this had the prestige of splendour and position and with the passage of time would gather associations which would prepare the way for it to become the one legitimate sanctuary of the land when centralization of the cultus was effected. Of less enduring importance were other marks of Solomon's ostentation. He gathered a large force of chariots, and the discovery of some of the stables for their horses at Megiddo has been already mentioned.

Notwithstanding the splendour of this reign, the kingdom of David had begun to disintegrate while Solomon was still on the throne. In the north Damascus became independent and was soon the head of a state which was long a thorn in Israel's side. The Philistine menace, which had welded Israel into a unity, was now removed, and discontent born of the oppressiveness of Solomon's rule was rife. A revolt was planned with prophetic support, but Jeroboam, who deserted the king's service to become its leader, was compelled to flee to Egypt for refuge. On the death of Solomon he returned, and when Rehoboam's folly added anger to discontent he placed himself at the head of the northern tribes, and the kingdom was disrupted. Egypt was not long in taking advantage of the situation. Shishak, so far from protecting the Jeroboam who had taken refuge at the Egyptian court, soon invaded both the Israelite kingdoms, harrying and plundering.

The south remained loyal to the house of David, and knew a stability the north never attained. Throughout its existence the northern kingdom saw frequent changes of dynasty, and until Omri made Samaria the capital the seat of the court was often moved. The relations between the two kingdoms constantly fluctuated and periods of mutual hostility alternated with periods of good relations. At times the south appealed to the king of Damascus to raid Israel to relieve the pressure of Israel upon Judah. Doubtless partly to strengthen his position against Damascus, Omri allied himself with Tyre. He also reconquered Moab, as we learn from the Moabite Stone (Plate 15), and made the northern kingdom stronger than it had yet been. His son's marriage to a Tyrian princess might have been a piece of wise statesmanship if that princess had been other than Jezebel proved herself to be. Flouting Israelite sentiment and arousing the antagonism of the prophets, and especially of the redoubtable Elijah, she proved herself to be the evil genius of the house of Omri. Her husband, Ahab, showed some signs of statesmanship when he showed clemency to the defeated and captured king of Damascus (1 Kings 20: 34); the explanation is found in an inscription of Shalmaneser III, but not in the Bible. For in 853 B.C., shortly after Ahab's treaty with Benhadad, the little western states met the Assyrian forces unitedly, and Ahab and Benhadad stood side by side with such effect that Assyrian advance was halted. But with the passing of the crisis unity ended, and Ahab lost his life in the battle for Ramoth-gilead.

The daughter of Ahab and Jezebel, who inherited her mother's spirit, had married the king of Judah, and it is clear that at the time of Ahab's death the southern king was under the dominance of his father-in-law. Before long the prophetic opposition to Jezebel swept the house of Omri away in a revolution that brought Jehu to the throne. Jezebel herself died ignominiously (2 Kings 9: 30 ff.). At the same time the royal house of Judah was almost wiped out. Jezebel's daughter, Athaliah, was beyond the reach of Jehu and immediately seized the power in Jerusalem, until the priest Jehoiada, who had protected Joash, the infant survivor of the line of David, publicly crowned him and restored the kingdom. The brief interlude of Athaliah's reign emphasizes the measure of stability of the southern dynasty in contrast to those of the northern kingdom.

It is curious to find that the same prophets who promoted the revolution against the house of Omri instigated a revolution in the kingdom of Damascus also; possibly this was to guard against Syrian exploitation of the Israelite weakness that would follow the fall of the Omrids, especially since that would entail the loss of the Tyrian alliance. In fact, however, Jehu soon felt the need of help against his Syrian neighbour and sent tribute to Shalmaneser (Plate 17) to secure his support by the threat of intervention against Damascus from the north. Little relief was obtained, and for many years Assyria took little part in the affairs of the west, so that the power of Damascus steadily grew. Towards the end of the ninth century, however, Syria was weakened by Assyrian attacks, and when a fresh period of Assyrian inactivity followed, Israel was able to enjoy a time of peace and prosperity such as she had not known for more than a century. In the north Jeroboam II was on the throne and in the south Uzziah, and throughout their long reigns the peace that prevailed between them gave them the opportunity to develop the strength and resources of their two kingdoms. The hollowness of the prosperity becomes clear when we perceive the grave social evils that marked the time, as they are reflected in the oracles of the eighth-century prophets, and within twenty-five years of the death of Jeroboam the northern kingdom had come to its end.

This was not wholly due to inner weakness. Tiglath-pileser had usurped the Assyrian throne and introduced a period of vigorous activity, marked also by the policy of deportation. Assyrian pressure on the west was now strong and continuous. The vacillation of Israelite policy and the repeated revolutions that took place, coupled with the complete lack of solidarity amongst the states of the west, ensured that no effective opposition should be offered. An attempt was made to revive a western alliance, and Syria and Israel tried to force Judah to join it, only to find Ahaz appeal for help to Assyria and bring upon them the attack which led to the fall of Damascus in 732 B.C. A decade later Samaria fell and the northern kingdom was no more. Many of its people were deported, to disappear from history.

Judah was now a buffer state between Assyria and Egypt, and the scene of constant Egyptian intrigue against Assyria. The fall of Samaria had not involved her, as she was a tributary state of Assyria at the time, but during the reign of Hezekiah she joined in a revolt, intended to synchronize with a revolt of Babylon in the east under Merodach-baladan. In preparation for this revolt Hezekiah strengthened the water supply of Jerusalem by constructing the Siloam tunnel to bring water through the rock into the pool in the lower part of the city (2 Kings 20: 20). He also put pressure upon the Philistine city of Ekron to come into the alliance and brought its king, Padi, a prisoner to Jerusalem. His religious reform was probably connected with his revolt, but its new feature was its centralization of worship in Jerusalem. Sennacherib was not long in moving his forces against the west, and quickly overran Judah. Of this campaign we have Sennacherib's account (Plate 16) as well as the Biblical story. Hezekiah yielded up Padi and came to terms with the Assyrian, who contented himself with demanding an indemnity and did not occupy

Jerusalem. Then he went to Lachish to meet the expected Egyptian attack, but ere it came plague broke out in his camp and he was forced to withdraw. The whole of Judah had suffered severely, and though Jerusalem had been spared the state was so crippled that the lesson was not easily forgotten. Hezekiah's successor, Manasseh, throughout his long reign continued to serve Assyria. Hezekiah's reform was short-lived, and all it had introduced was abandoned. In fairness to Manasseh it should be remembered that Assyrian power was at its highest at this time, and Egypt was twice invaded and conquered, though it did not remain for long a part of the Assyrian empire. Indeed, when Manasseh died that empire was approaching its downfall, and within a few years it had sunk from its glory into ruin.

The death of Ashurbanipal was the signal for a new revolt in Babylon under Nabopolassar, and the western states had new dreams of independence. Josiah was now on the throne of Jerusalem, and he planned a fresh revolt and carried through a reform of religion once more, embodying again the principle of centralization, but this time based on the Book of the Law found in the Temple (2 Kings 22: 8 f.). Assyria was in no position to intervene in the west, since she was fighting for her life in the east. Now Egypt abandoned her traditional anti-Assyrian policy and allied herself with the falling empire. But all in vain. In 612 B.C. Nineveh fell and the capital was transferred to Haran; but two years later Haran fell and the Assyrian empire was annexed by the conquerors. Nebuchadrezzar, the son of Nabopolassar, led the army of his father and sought to consolidate the new rule in the conquered territory before making a fresh advance, while Pharaoh Neco occupied the former Assyrian territory west of the Euphrates. Josiah's dreams

Plate 15 left

The Moabite Stone (recording King Mesha's revolt)

Plate 16 right

Prism of Sennacherib (recording his campaign against Jerusalem)

Plate 17 left

Obelisk of Shalmaneser (recording Jehu's tribute)

Plate 18 right

One of the Lachish Letters (from the time of Zedekiah)

Plate 19

Above: Bethlehem (from the south)
Below: The Cliffs at Caesarea Philippi

Plate 20

Plate 2

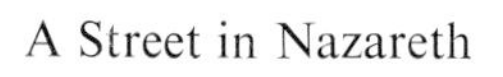

A Street in Nazareth

Plate 22

Above: Mount Tabor
Below: The Mount of Olives (from the Temple site)

Plate 23

Plate 24

Plate 25

Plate 26

Above: Athens, the Acropolis with the Parthenon
Below: The Ruins of Ephesus

Plate 27

Plate 28

of independence vanished, and his attempt to resist Neco ended in his death at Megiddo.

In 605 B.C., however, Nebuchadrezzar defeated Neco at the battle of Carchemish, and the Egyptian forces hastily withdrew to Egypt, with Nebuchadrezzar hot in pursuit through Syria and Palestine, which he added to the Neo-Babylonian empire. Four years later Egypt tried to recover her position and a fierce battle was fought in the south. Throughout the remaining years of the kingdom of Judah, Egypt continued to foster hopes of freedom from Babylon. Jehoiakim, who had been placed upon the throne by Neco as one who was friendly to Egypt, never gave real loyalty to Babylon, and at the time of his death was engaged in revolt. Before the Babylonian army appeared on the scene he himself had died, and his young son, Jehoiachin, seeing the hopelessness of resistance, capitulated and was taken a prisoner to Babylon, where he languished in captivity for nearly forty years. With him numbers of his people were carried into exile.

Jehoiachin was replaced on the throne by his weak uncle, Zedekiah, who after a few years succumbed to the intrigues of Egypt and shared in a new western revolt. This time Jerusalem was invested and after a desperate resistance was taken. The Temple was destroyed and further numbers of people were removed into exile in Babylonia. Judah became a province of Babylon, and the Davidic monarchy had reached its inglorious end. From the book of Jeremiah we learn something of the unhappy tensions that prevailed in Jerusalem in the closing years of the kingdom, and the Lachish Letters tell us something of the tensions that marked life in the garrisons that stubbornly continued the struggle almost to the fall of Jerusalem.

—7—

From the Exile to the Advent

WE have little record of events in Palestine between the Exile and the Return. We learn of fresh disorders when Gedaliah, who had been made governor by Nebuchadrezzar, was murdered (2 Kings 25: 22 ff.), but of the subsequent events we know nothing. Nor do we have much information of the exiles in Babylon. Before the fall of Jerusalem the first exiles had dreamed of a speedy return, but Jeremiah had urged them to settle down in their new homes and to realize that they were there for a long time (Jer. 29: 4 ff.). Gradually numbers of them did settle down, and when later the opportunity to return came many did not avail themselves of it. Amongst the exiles was Ezekiel, whose oracles have been preserved for us, and who later envisaged a new Temple with a carefully regulated cultus and priesthood. The exiles cherished the memory of their own country, and in their settlements developed a loyalty to their faith which had too seldom been shown in former days. Probably it was here, where they were denied the opportunity to observe the cultus, that they gathered for fellowship and prayer and laid the foundations for the worship of the synagogue, which was later found in Palestine and wherever companies of Jews could gather throughout the world.

The greatness of the Neo-Babylonian empire passed with the death of Nebuchadrezzar. A few years of disorder led to the revolt of Nabonidus, in whose reign a new world situation arose. To the east lay the empire of Media, which had been allied with Babylon in the assault upon Assyria. But now Cyrus, king of Anshan, became king of Persia, and then rose against his suzerain, the king of Media, and converted the Median empire into the Persian. With astonishing rapidity he conquered and annexed the Lydian kingdom of Croesus, and a few years later swallowed up the Neo-Babylonian empire. For most of his reign Nabonidus lived at Tema, leaving his son Belshazzar to administer the kingdom. Amongst the Jewish exiles the nameless prophet whom we know as Deutero-Isaiah perceived the significance of what was happening, and encouraged his people with the promise of restoration to their own land. But although Cyrus gave them permission to return when he occupied Babylon, the numbers of those who did so were not large, and though they appear to have laid the foundations of the Second Temple, in accordance with the permission of Cyrus, they were too immersed in the problems of resettlement to continue the work.

Cyrus was followed by Cambyses, who carried Persian arms into Egypt. From the Elephantine Papyri we learn with surprise that he found a Jewish colony far up the Nile, with their own temple, and of this colony we have much information down to the end of the fifth century. Cambyses did not return from Egypt, and immediately after his death it seemed as if the Persian empire would fall to pieces. Before setting out for Egypt Cambyses had put his own brother, Smerdis, to death, but one Gaumata, giving himself out to be Smerdis, now claimed the throne. Throughout the empire there was revolt, each district seeking to achieve independence once more. Then Darius Hystaspis, who though not the heir to the throne was related to the royal house, assumed the leadership and gradually reduced the empire to obedience, and then organized it more firmly than it had been hitherto. It was this situation which provided the setting for the work of Haggai and Zechariah and for the rebuilding of the Temple. The governor of Jerusalem was Zerubbabel, of the line of David, and the Jews shared the widespread hope of renewed independence. As in the past, the revival of national hopes was coupled with religious revival, and the work of rebuilding the Temple was now seriously undertaken. Before it was completed Zerubbabel disappeared, probably because the land was brought again under Persian sway, but the rebuilding of the Temple, which had been authorized by Cyrus, was not interfered with in spite of Samaritan intrigues.

Then once more the curtain falls, and we have little knowledge of the period down to the middle of the following century. In the reign of Artaxerxes I there was an abortive attempt to rebuild the walls of Jerusalem, but this was thwarted by Samaritan jealousy of Jerusalem (Ezra 4: 7 ff.). The work was forcibly stopped, and doubtless what had been rebuilt was broken down. Probably it was news of this that so saddened Nehemiah (Neh. 1: 4). Yet seizing his opportunity he obtained permission from the king to lead a body of exiles back with authority to rebuild the walls. Laying his plans with secrecy and skill, he carried the work through with such swiftness that there was no time for his foes to make fresh trouble at the court before it was completed. At this time Sanballat was the governor of Samaria. His opposition seems to have been political rather than religious, since he was a worshipper of Yahweh, and a few years later we find the son of the High Priest in Jerusalem married to his daughter (Neh. 13: 28). That there was no final breach between Jews and Samaritans yet is clear from the fact that when, towards the end of the fifth century, the Temple at Elephantine was destroyed by the Egyptians, the Jews there appealed both to Sanballat's sons and to the priests of Jerusalem to use their good offices to secure authority for its rebuilding.

As has been said in an earlier chapter, it is probable that the work of Ezra belonged to the reign of Artaxerxes II at the beginning of the fourth century B.C. Egypt had recently become independent of Persia, and the king may have been anxious to ensure that what was now a frontier state should be friendly to its rulers.

From this time to the rise of Alexander and the fall of the Persian empire we have little knowledge of the history of Palestine. Alexander visited Jerusalem, where he was welcomed by the High Priest, and when he founded the city of Alexandria many Jews settled there. Indeed, from this time on Alexandria became an important centre of the Jews of the Diaspora. Palestine passed from the Persian to the Greek empire, and when Alexander died and his generals fell to carving out for themselves dominions until gradually settled divisions of the empire emerged, the Jews found themselves for a century under the rule of the Ptolemies, who controlled Egypt. Seleucus I, who established the dynasty that ruled Syria, Asia Minor, and Babylonia, claimed that Palestine should really have been his, and it remained a bone of contention between the two Hellenistic powers throughout the third century, until in 198 B.C., after the battle of Panion, Antiochus III annexed it to his own realm. To some of the Jews the change was not unwelcome. The Ptolemaic rule had not been harsh, and Jewish legend claimed that the Greek version of the Pentateuch, which was made in Alexandria in the middle of the third century B.C., had been prepared under royal patronage. But by the end of the century dissensions had appeared amongst the Jews between the rival houses of the Oniads and the Tobiads. The latter had secured from Ptolemy the tax-farming rights hitherto held by the High Priest, who was of the Oniad house. Hence the Oniads welcomed the transfer to Seleucid rule in the hope that they would recover their rights. In this they were mistaken. The Tobiads were ready to transfer their allegiance wherever their interests dictated, and they soon stood higher in the favour of their new masters than did their rivals.

Soon after the transfer of Palestine to the Seleucids, Antiochus III was involved in war with Rome, and after the defeat of the battle of Magnesia in 190 B.C., he lost the control of Asia Minor, and was forced to pay a large indemnity to Rome. His successor therefore inherited a state impoverished by war and reduced in extent, and in addition was compelled to find an annual payment for Rome, where his brother was kept as a hostage. In common with all his subjects, therefore, the Jews soon found that taxation was oppressive, and many began to sigh for the Ptolemaic rule. The situation was complicated by religious questions. From the time of Alexander the influence of the Greek way of life had been felt, and while some Jews yielded to it, others had become increasingly rigid in their adherence to their own way of life, so that the Oniads became the symbols of religious loyalty as well as the leaders of anti-Seleucid sympathies. When an attempt was made to rob the Temple to supply Seleucus IV with funds, all this was accentuated.

Then Seleucus was murdered by his minister Heliodorus, and his infant son was proclaimed king by the murderer, who planned to seize the reality of power. Antiochus IV, the brother of Seleucus who had by now been released from being a hostage, his place being taken by Demetrius, the rightful heir to the throne, speedily appeared in Syria and claimed the throne. Soon he had eliminated Heliodorus and also his infant nephew, and established himself in Syria. Next he sought an excuse to intervene in the affairs of Egypt, where two of his nephews were quarrelling for the throne. But neither desired the " protection " their young cousin had had, and they quickly made up their quarrel and agreed to rule jointly. When Antiochus made a further effort to intervene, they appealed to Rome for protection, and Antiochus, who had by now led an army into Egypt, was foiled and humiliated by the Roman envoy and compelled to withdraw from the land.

When Antiochus came to Jerusalem, sore at his humiliation, he found occasion to vent his feelings on the disaffected Jews. There were some who had from the first questioned his title to the throne. Their opposition to the Seleucids had been strengthened by royal interference with the appointment of the High Priest. Onias had been replaced by his brother Jason, who was of the Hellenistic party, and Onias himself had been killed. But Jason soon yielded the office to Menelaus, who was not even of the priestly tribe, but who ingratiated himself into the royal favour (2 Macc. 4: 23 ff.). The policy of Hellenization was pressed forward and the rival parties in Jerusalem became ever more antagonistic to one another. Political and religious issues became more and more closely intertwined, and disaffection continued to mount. Hence Antiochus decided to attack the religious root of the opposition, in the belief that if this were dealt with it would wither and die. He therefore proscribed all the practices of the Jewish law (1 Macc. 1: 44 ff.). Circumcision was forbidden, and the possession of the sacred books was made a capital offence.

The Temple was defiled and turned into a shrine of Zeus, and people were compelled to eat swine's flesh. But the king had underestimated the strength of Jewish loyalty to their faith, and before long the standard of revolt was raised by an aged priest, and the Maccabaean rebellion had begun.

At first this rebellion was led by Judas, the son of the priest who had precipitated it. Antiochus himself had gone to the east, and his officers had little measure of the situation. Hence Judas won some successes by guerilla tactics, and three years after the Temple had been defiled it was again in his possession, though the citadel was still held by the king's forces. The Temple was cleansed and rededicated. Soon afterwards the death of Antiochus led to a period of constant turmoil in the Seleucid kingdom. Judas was killed in battle in 161 B.C., but he was succeeded by his brother Jonathan, and on the death of Jonathan by another brother, Simon. By offering their support to the highest bidder among the contestants for power in Syria they strengthened their position, and finally secured Jewish independence and established the dynasty which became known as the Hasmonaeans. They held the dual office of High Priest and civil leader of the community, and finally assumed the title of king, save during the period when the civil power was held by a woman, when it was divorced from the priesthood.

At some time during the second century B.C. the Jewish parties of Pharisees and Sadducees came into being. The Pharisees were the heirs of the religious enthusiasts who had supported the Maccabees, while the Sadducees inherited something of the spirit of the Hellenistic party, though they were less extreme than the Hellenists who had supported Antiochus. There was no longer any uestion of disloyalty to the faith of Judaism, though was a breach of the Law when the Hasmonaeans, who ere of a priestly family but not of the high priestly ne, assumed the high priesthood. Into the struggles f these two parties this is not the place to go. Tension eveloped between them, and in the reign of Alexander nnaeus the Pharisees went so far as to invite Seleucid d against the king, with the result that Jannaeus had ght hundred of them crucified.

Meanwhile, at some time during the second century, nother group of Jews, more rigid than the Pharisees, ad been formed. They too seem to have been heirs f the stricter party of Maccabaean times, but they were ore uncompromising than the Pharisees. They called emselves the "sons of Zadok", and seem to have een unbending supporters of the true high priestly line. hey withdrew from the Temple services and established emselves as a kind of monastic community near the ead Sea at *Qumrân*. Here were their headquarters, ough there were other groups of the same sect scatred throughout the land. They had all things in mmon and spent much time in the study of the Scripres, and at their centre in *Qumrân* large numbers of pies of the sacred texts were made. In addition, rther texts, reflecting the history, thought, and practices the sect, were composed, and it is the remains of the rary of this sect that have been found in recent years the Dead Sea Scrolls.

Towards the middle of the first century B.C. family arrels amongst the Hasmonaeans developed, and these ere soon caught up in world events through the disnsions of the Roman empire. Pompey came to Jerulem to decide the issues amongst the Jews and to nex Palestine to the Roman empire. Thereafter the

dominant figure on the Jerusalem scene was Herod, a
Idumaean, who skilfully pursued his own interes
through all the changes of the Roman Civil War, unt
he was given the title of king and left to win his kin
dom for himself. This he was not long in doing, ar
thereafter he continued to rule over the Jews until 4 B.
To the Jews he was always an alien, and though he di
much to protect their interests he never won their grat
tude. He began the rebuilding of the Temple, but h
had no deep interest in their religion and with equ
readiness erected other buildings which they could n
approve. His character was marked by cunning ar
cruelty, and his own family had frequent experien
of this. His wife and children were executed with a
little compunction as any of his subjects who incurr
his anger.

Not long before the death of Herod there was bo
in a Bethlehem inn the Babe whose birth is recognize
to mark the great division of history. In vain Herc
sought to kill Him in His infancy; others later succeede
in nailing Him to a Cross, but not before His work w
finished.

—8—

Darkness and Dawn

ON the death of Herod his kingdom was divided. It had been Herod's wish that his son Archelaus
ıould succeed him, but Caesar decided otherwise. A
ewish embassy prayed for the abolition of the kingship,
ıd Caesar so far acceded to this that he did not grant
ıe title of king. He assigned to Archelaus the rule of
ıdaea, Samaria, and Idumaea, with the title of tetrarch
ıd the prospect of elevation to the royal dignity later.
he remainder of Herod's kingdom went to Antipas,
ıe brother of Archelaus, and Philip, his half-brother,
ıch with the title of tetrarch. The rule of Archelaus
sted for ten years. Never popular with his subjects,
contrived to anger them until they petitioned Rome
have him removed from office, and he was banished
Gaul. Thereafter Roman procurators were appointed,
f whom Pontius Pilate, who took office in A.D. 26, is
ıe one who most concerns the student of the Bible.
hroughout the ministry of Jesus he filled the office of
rocurator, and he it was who authorized the Crucifixion
f our Lord, after a futile pretence of absolving himself
responsibility. He took little account of Jewish
ısceptibilities, and as little of Samaritan, and in the end
was removed from office on the complaint of the
ımaritans.

Meanwhile Antipas continued to rule in Galilee.
'iser than Archelaus, he yet failed to please his sub-
cts, and finally brought about his own undoing. He
arried the daughter of the Arabian king, Aretas, but
ter abandoned her for Herodias, and for this conduct
was castigated by John the Baptist. This in turn led

to the arrest and imprisonment of John, and later t
his beheading at the wish of Herodias. Herodias wa
indeed, the evil genius of Antipas. The treatment
the daughter of Aretas aroused her father to attac
Antipas, who suffered a severe defeat. Moreove
Herodias desired for her husband the title of king, sin
by now Herod Agrippa I had succeeded Philip and als
Lysanias (who had ruled over territory east of the Jorda
and farther north) and had been given the title of kin
Herodias accordingly urged her husband to go to Ron
to secure the same title for himself. But Agrippa sowe
suspicion of Antipas, who instead of returning a kin
lost the title he had, and was banished to Gaul, h
domain being added to that of Agrippa. Later th
procuratorship of Judaea was superseded, and Judae
and Samaria were added to the realm of Agrippa. Th
kingdom of Herod was now restored, though Agripp
like Herod, was responsible to Rome for his rule.

Within the period thus briefly sketched lay the minist
of Jesus. Born at Bethlehem (Plate 19), He was carrie
in infancy to Egypt and on His return He was broug
up at the Galilean village of Nazareth (Plate 21). W
know of but one visit to Jerusalem before the beginnin
of His ministry. That ministry was exercised largely i
Galilee, though visits to some of the Jerusalem feas
are recorded. Capernaum and Bethsaida, on the shor
of the Sea of Galilee (Plate 14), heard His utterance
and Cana of Galilee witnessed the first of His miracle
Sometimes He crossed to the east of the lake, and the
the crowds followed Him and were fed with the loav
and fishes. Once He came to Jacob's Well, not far fro
Samaria, and there He held converse with the woma
of Samaria. He came to Caesarea Philippi (Plate 20
and from that time prepared His disciples for His suffe

ing and death (Matt. 16: 13 ff.). On His last visit to Jerusalem (Plate 12) He passed through Jericho. Bethany and Emmaus are associated with His story, and the Garden of Gethsemane on the Mount of Olives (Plate 23), separated from Jerusalem by the Kidron valley (Plate 11), and above all that other hill, called Calvary.

Then the New Testament needs a wider canvas for its scene. The followers of Jesus were found at Jerusalem, and then at Samaria (Plate 10), Caesarea, Damascus (Plate 24) and Antioch (Plate 25), and it was at Antioch that they were first called Christians. From Antioch Paul and Barnabas set out on their first missionary journey to Cyprus and Asia Minor, and later Paul with other companions went through Asia Minor and into Europe, to Philippi, Thessalonica, Athens (Plate 26) and Corinth, and back into Asia Minor to Ephesus (Plate 27). Returning to Jerusalem from his third journey, he was there arrested and imprisoned in Caesarea, and finally sent for trial to Rome (Plate 28). It is often observed that the Roman empire, with its internal peace and good communications, gave Paul an opportunity to spread the Gospel that he could not have found in an earlier age. The empire of Alexander had left as its enduring legacy the spread of Greek culture and of the Greek language, which was invaluable to the early Church. It should also be remembered that the Jews of the Diaspora were of the first importance. Reference has already been made to the Jews of Alexandria. But in the post-exilic age groups of Jews were found scattered throughout the Mediterranean world, and synagogues and places of prayer were found in countless localities. Many proselytes had embraced Judaism, and other Gentiles were deeply interested in the life and teaching of the Jews, though they were not committed so far as to become proselytes. Wherever Paul went with the Gospel, he was opposed and persecuted by Jews. Yet it was to Jews that he owed his first opportunity to preach the Gospel in town after town, and it was in the synagogues that he delivered his first message. When he was driven out of the synagogues, he was often accompanied by those he had first impressed there.

The ministry of Paul carries us beyond the time of Herod Agrippa I, who died in A.D. 44. His only son was Herod Agrippa II, but he did not succeed to his father's throne. He was given a small kingdom in the north, to which were added later the territory that had once been the tetrarchy of Philip, and some other districts. He was given some authority over the Temple, however, and had a residence in Jerusalem, and it was before him that Paul presented his case, after he had appealed to Rome (Acts 25 f.). Judaea was once again placed under the rule of procurators, two of whom figure in the New Testament story. These were Felix and Festus.

By this time the situation in Palestine was growing tense and critical. The reader of the Gospels is aware that amongst the Jews there were some who accepted Roman rule and some who bitterly resented it. The more extreme of the latter were the Zealots, a party that came into existence early in the Roman period, and that became increasingly pledged to throw off the Roman yoke. The Messianic hope had become linked with the thought of political revolution, and it was for that reason that Jesus deprecated the use of the title Messiah—which in its Greek form of Christ has become His commonest title. Hostility to Rome mounted more and more, until in the procuratorship of Florus, who came to Judaea in A.D. 64, open revolt broke out. The course of the war cannot be followed here. The rebels split into rival groups, which fought one another with a ferocity equal to that they showed towards their common foe. At one time the Roman armies were commanded by Vespasian, who was summoned from his post to assume the purple, and in the end Jerusalem fell to Titus. The city was defended with desperate tenacity after all hope was clearly vain, and when it fell the Temple fell with it and was utterly destroyed, never to be rebuilt to this day. Its site is occupied by a Moslem mosque (Plate 8).

Meanwhile, at *Qumrân*, the Romans destroyed the settlement of the sectaries mentioned above. It is probable that these sectaries had developed into the Essenes, of whom we have accounts in the writings of Philo, Pliny and Josephus, though they are unmentioned in the New Testament. Amongst the works treasured by the Qumrân sect was a War Scroll, which describes the war that should destroy earthly kingdoms and establish the world-wide sway of the Children of Light. Yet for years the Essenes had lived a peaceful life of contemplation and study, without neglect of work for their sustenance, and in the pages of Josephus they appear as pacifists. It would seem curious, therefore, that the Romans should destroy their centre in A.D. 68. One of the Essenes had become a commander in the rebel army, and we learn that the Romans tortured many of the Essenes in the most cruel way. Clearly the Romans regarded the Essenes as actively sympathetic towards the Zealots. It may well have been that they believed that the time which the War Scroll had taught them to expect had come, and that they gave active help to the Zealots. Some colour is given to this by the presence amongst their manuscripts of a copper scroll which recorded vast quantities of buried treasure. It has been conjectured that this was Temple treasure, which had been removed from Jerusalem and hidden. If so, it could hardly be doubted that the sectaries of *Qumrân* must have been in some way associated with the Zealots in Jerusalem. However that may be, before the Qumrân centre was destroyed, its manuscripts were deposited in many of the caves in the neighbourhood, to astonish the world in the middle of the twentieth century when they were brought to light, many of them in the tiniest fragments. As has been said earlier, some of these texts were composed by members of the sect. More are fragments of copies of the Scriptures. It was by those Scriptures that Israel made her enduring contribution to the world, and through all the intervening centuries they have been cherished by multitudes of men as the lively oracles of God. The Jews, who became wanderers, with no country of their own till recent years, were the people of the Book, for the Scriptures of the Old Testament were their supreme glory. Christians, too, cherished this Book and carried it wherever they went, translating it into countless languages, and to it they added the New Testament, which tells of the culmination of the revelation of the God of the Old Testament in the Person of Christ. The Temple might pass, and without it the Jews have nourished their faith through the ages. For the Christian it might pass, not because the hand of circumstance destroyed it, but because its sacrifices were superseded in the supreme sacrifice for the world on the Cross of Calvary. Before the darkness of the disaster of A.D. 70 fell upon Jerusalem, the Dayspring from on high had appeared and already the new faith which had been born from Judaism and which knew no boundaries of race or nation had begun to go forth to all the world

MAPS

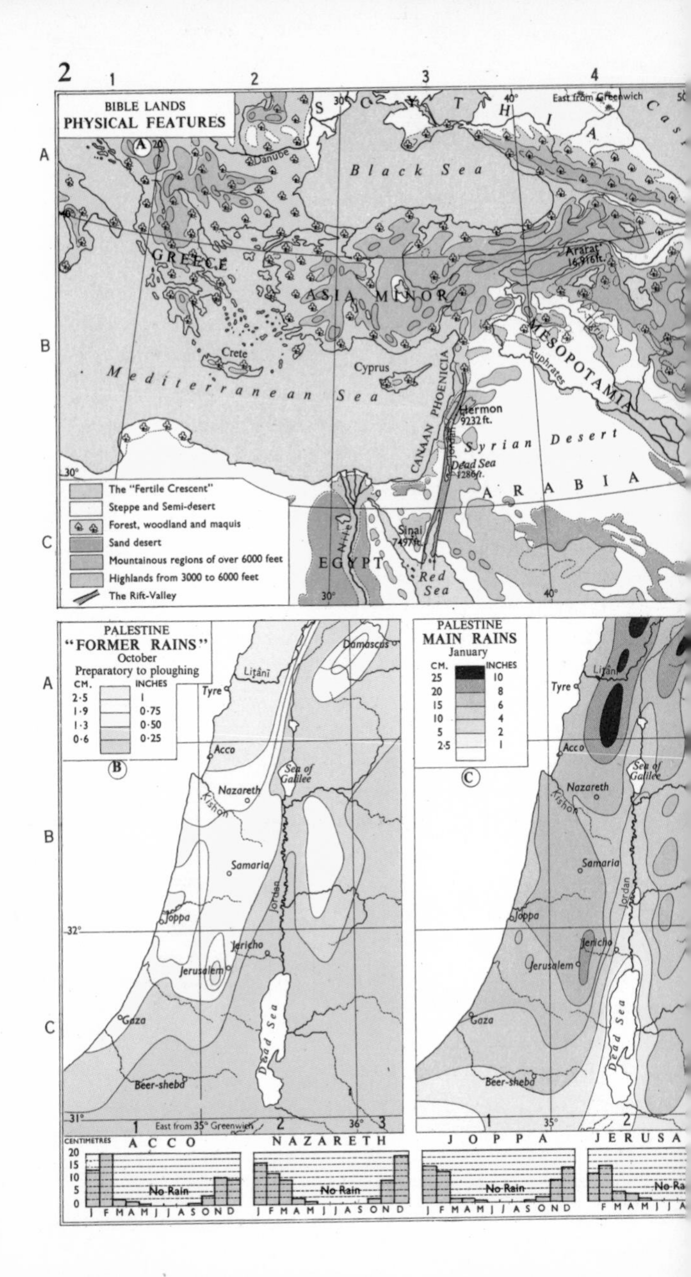
BIBLE LANDS
PHYSICAL FEATURES
The "Fertile Crescent"
Steppe and Semi-desert
Forest, woodland and maquis
Sand desert
Mountainous regions of over 6000 feet
Highlands from 3000 to 6000 feet
The Rift-Valley
East from Greenwich
GREECE
ASIA MINOR
MESOPOTAMIA
ARABIA
EGYPT
CANAAN PHOENICIA
Black Sea
Mediterranean Sea
Syrian Desert
Red Sea
Danube
Crete
Cyprus
Hermon 9232 ft.
Dead Sea 1286 ft.
Ararat 16,916 ft.
Sinai 7497 ft.
Nile
Euphrates
Tigris
Jordan
PALESTINE
"FORMER RAINS"
October
Preparatory to ploughing
CM. INCHES
2·5 1
1·9 0·75
1·3 0·50
0·6 0·25
PALESTINE
MAIN RAINS
January
CM. INCHES
25 10
20 8
15 6
10 4
5 2
2·5 1
Damascus
Litani
Tyre
Acco
Sea of Galilee
Nazareth
Kishon
Samaria
Joppa
Jericho
Jerusalem
Gaza
Beer-sheba
Dead Sea
East from 35° Greenwich
CENTIMETRES
ACCO
NAZARETH
JOPPA
JERUSA
No Rain
J F M A M J J A S O N D

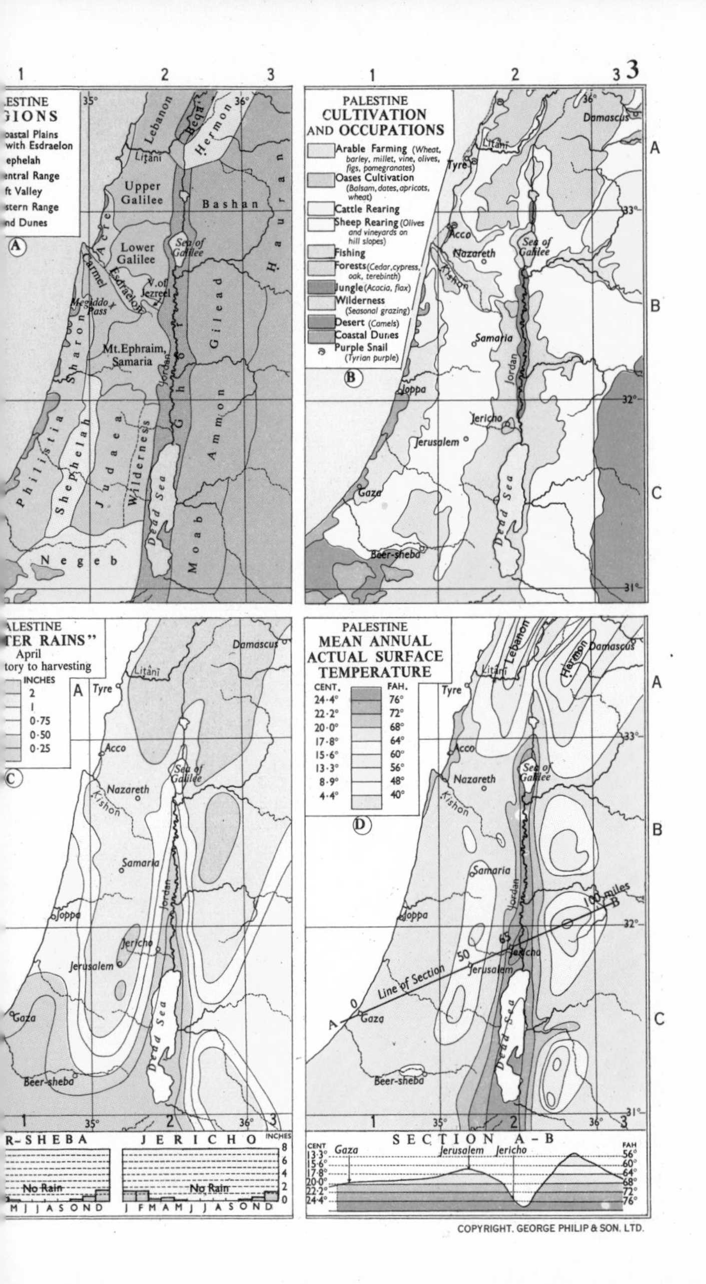
PALESTINE
CULTIVATION AND OCCUPATIONS
Arable Farming (Wheat, barley, millet, vine, olives, figs, pomegranates)
Oases Cultivation (Balsam, dates, apricots, wheat)
Cattle Rearing
Sheep Rearing (Olives and vineyards on hill slopes)
Fishing
Forests (Cedar, cypress, oak, terebinth)
Jungle (Acacia, flax)
Wilderness (Seasonal grazing)
Desert (Camels)
Coastal Dunes
Purple Snail (Tyrian purple)
B
PALESTINE
MEAN ANNUAL ACTUAL SURFACE TEMPERATURE
CENT. FAH.
24·4° 76°
22·2° 72°
20·0° 68°
17·8° 64°
15·6° 60°
13·3° 56°
8·9° 48°
4·4° 40°
D
Upper Galilee
Lower Galilee
Bashan
Gilead
Ammon
Moab
Negeb
Judaea
Wilderness
Shephelah
Philistia
Sharon
Carmel
Mt.Ephraim, Samaria
Megiddo Pass
Esdraelon
V. of Jezreel
Lebanon
Beqa'
Hermon
Hauran
Damascus
Tyre
Acco
Nazareth
Kishon
Samaria
Joppa
Jericho
Jerusalem
Gaza
Beer-sheba
Sea of Galilee
Dead Sea
Jordan
Litani
Line of Section
100 miles
SECTION A – B
Gaza
Jerusalem
Jericho
No Rain
JERICHO
INCHES

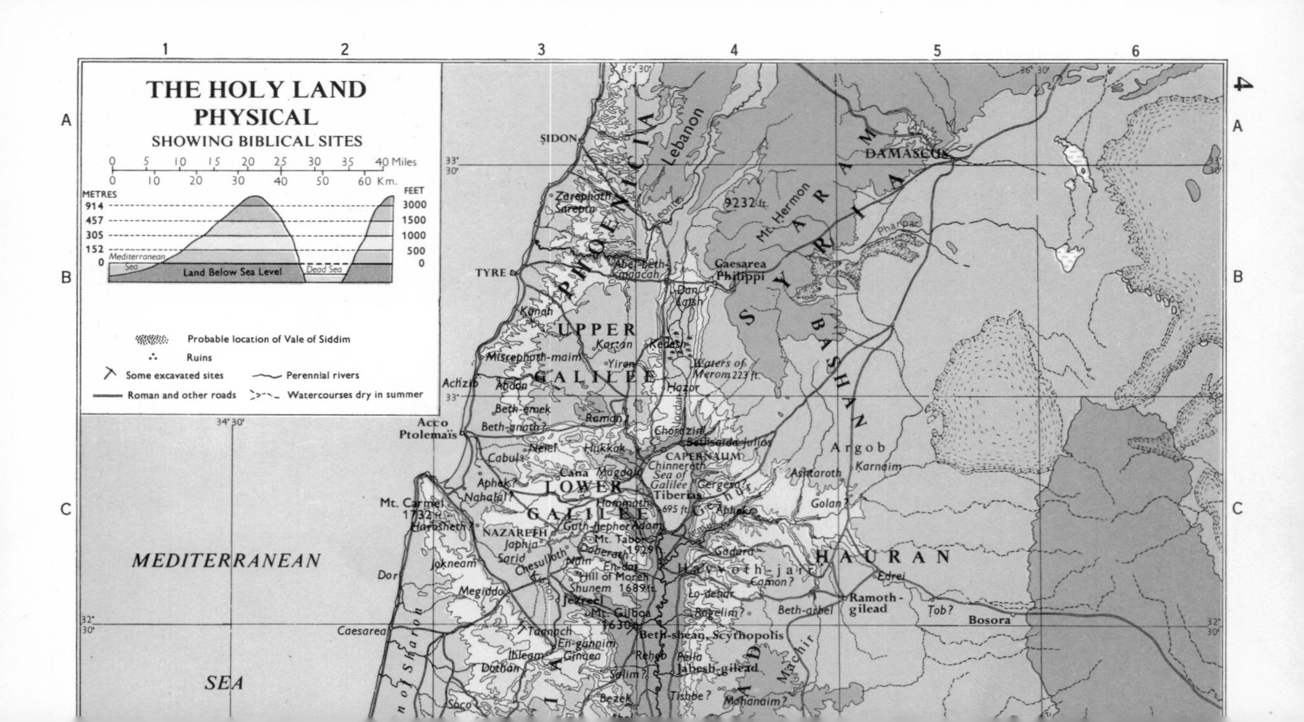
THE HOLY LAND
PHYSICAL
SHOWING BIBLICAL SITES
Miles
Km.
METRES
FEET
Mediterranean Sea
Land Below Sea Level
Dead Sea
Probable location of Vale of Siddim
Ruins
Some excavated sites
Perennial rivers
Roman and other roads
Watercourses dry in summer
SIDON
Zarephath
Sarepta
PHOENICIA
Lebanon
Leontes
DAMASCUS
ARAM
SYRIA
Mt. Hermon
9232 ft.
Pharpar
TYRE
Abel-beth-maacah
Caesarea Philippi
Dan
Laish
Kanah
UPPER
GALILEE
Kartan
Kedesh
Misrephoth-maim
Yiron
Waters of Merom 223 ft.
Achzib
Abdon
Hazor
BASHAN
Beth-emek
Ramah
Jordan
Acco
Ptolemaïs
Beth-anath?
Chorazin
Bethsaida-Julias
Neiel
Hukkok
CAPERNAUM
Argob
Cabul
Cana
Magdala
Chinnereth
Sea of Galilee
Gergesa?
Ashtaroth
Karnaim
Aphek?
LOWER
GALILEE
Tiberias
Geshur
Mt. Carmel
1732 ft.
Nahalal?
Hammath
695 ft.
Aphek
Golan?
Harosheth
NAZARETH
Gath-hepher
Adam
Japhia
Mt. Tabor
Daberath
1929
Gadara
HAURAN
MEDITERRANEAN
Sarid
Chesulloth
Nain
En-dor
Havvoth-jair
Jokneam
Hill of Moreh
Camon?
Edrei
Dor
Shunem
1689 ft.
Megiddo
Jezreel
Lo-debar
Ramoth-gilead
Mt. Gilboa
1630 ft.
Rogelim?
Beth-arbel
Tob?
Bosora
Caesarea
Taanach
Beth-shean, Scythopolis
En-gannim
Ibleam
Ginaea
Rehob
Pella
Machir
Plain of Sharon
Dothan
Salim?
Jabesh-gilead
GILEAD
SEA
Bezek
Tishbe?
Mahanaim?
Soco
1
2
3
4
5
6
A
B
C

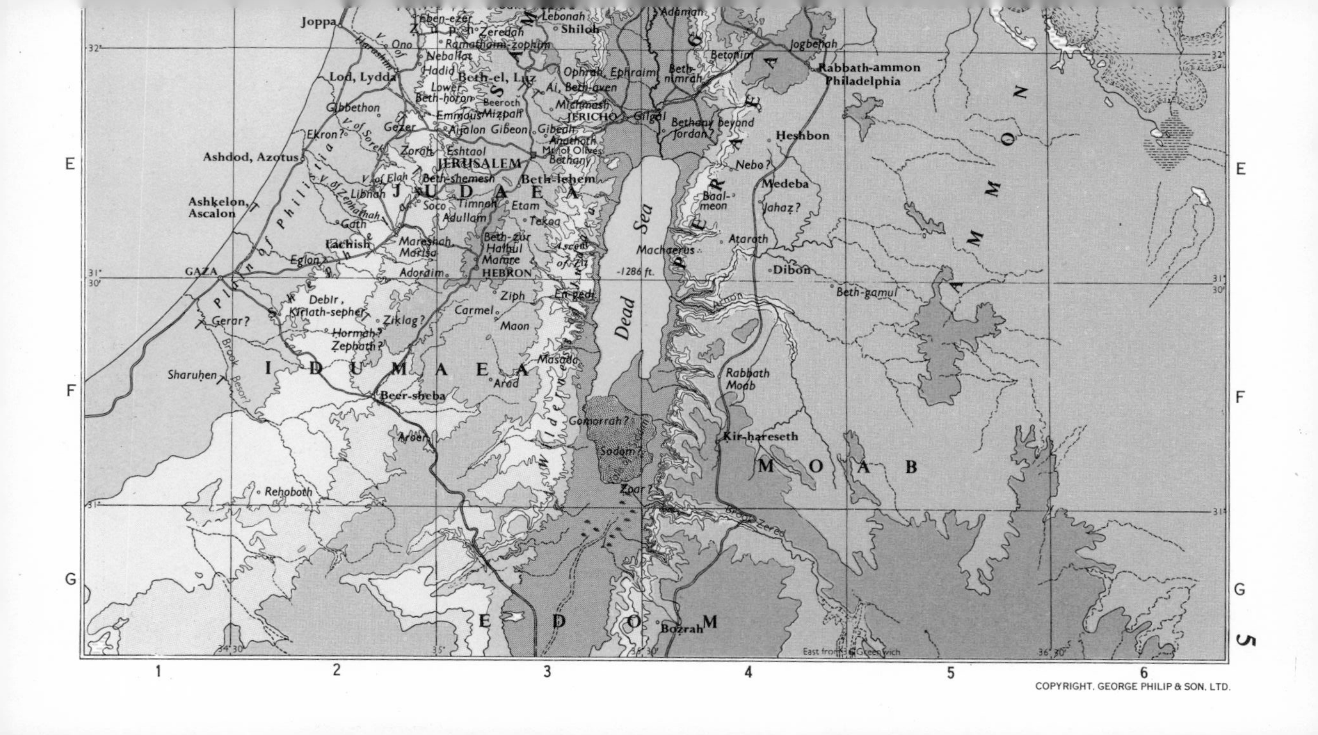
Joppa
Lod, Lydda
Gibbethon
Ekron?
Ashdod, Azotus
Ashkelon, Ascalon
GAZA
Gerar?
Sharuhen
Rehoboth
Gezer
Zorah
Eshtaol
JERUSALEM
Beth-shemesh
Libnah
Soco
Timnah
Adullam
Gath
Lachish
Eglon
Mareshah, Marisa
Adoraim
Debir, Kiriath-sepher
Ziklag?
Hormah? Zephath?
Beer-sheba
Aroer
Beth-zur
Halhul
Mamre
HEBRON
Ziph
Carmel
Maon
Arad
Masada
En-gedi
Etam
Tekoa
Beth-lehem
Bethany
Anathoth
Gibeah
Gibeon
Aijalon
Emmaus
Mizpah
Beeroth
Lower Beth-horon
Hadid
Neballat
Ono
Ramathaim-zophim
Zeredah
Lebonah
Shiloh
Beth-el, Luz
Ai, Beth-aven
Michmash
JERICHO
Gilgal
Ophrah, Ephraim
Beth-nimrah
Betonim
Adamah
Jogbehah
Rabbath-ammon
Philadelphia
Bethany beyond Jordan?
Heshbon
Nebo?
Medeba
Baal-meon
Jahaz?
Ataroth
Machaerus
Dibon
Beth-gamul
Arnon
Rabbath Moab
Kir-hareseth
Brook Zered
Zoar?
Sodom?
Gomorrah?
Bozrah
Dead Sea
-1286 ft.
Brook Besor?
JUDAEA
IDUMAEA
PERAEA
AMMON
MOAB
EDOM
SAMARIA
Wilderness of Judaea
East from Greenwich
COPYRIGHT, GEORGE PHILIP & SON, LTD.

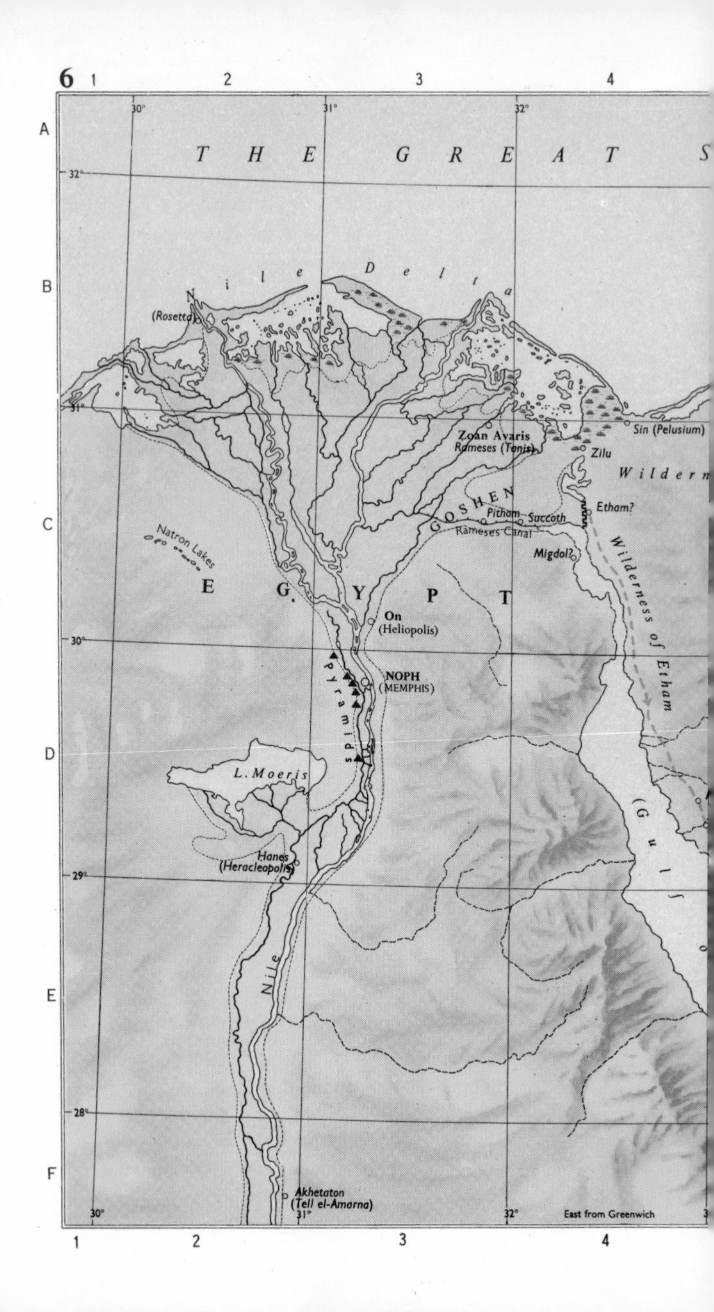
THE GREAT S
Nile Delta
(Rosetta)
Sin (Pelusium)
Zoan Avaris
Rameses (Tanis)
Zilu
Wilderm
GOSHEN
Pithom
Succoth
Etham?
Rameses Canal
Migdol?
Natron Lakes
EGYPT
Wilderness of Etham
On
(Heliopolis)
NOPH
(MEMPHIS)
Pyramids
L. Moeris
Hanes
(Heracleopolis)
(Gulf o
Nile
Akhetaton
(Tell el-Amarna)
East from Greenwich
30°
31°
32°
29°
28°
A
B
C
D
E
F
1
2
3
4

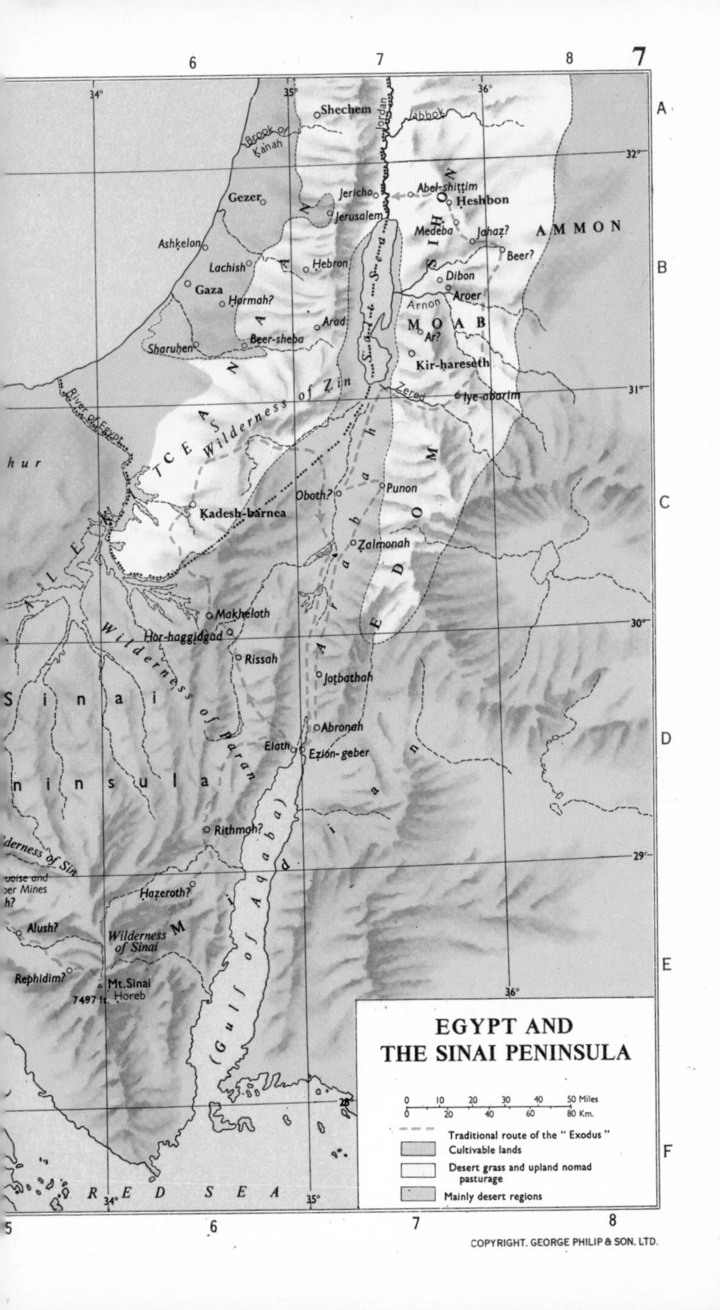
EGYPT AND
THE SINAI PENINSULA
0 10 20 30 40 50 Miles
0 20 40 60 80 Km.
Traditional route of the " Exodus "
Cultivable lands
Desert grass and upland nomad pasturage
Mainly desert regions
Shechem
Jordan
Jabbok
Brook of Kanah
Gezer
Jericho
Jerusalem
Abel-shittim
Heshbon
Medeba
Jahaz?
AMMON
Beer?
Ashkelon
Lachish
Hebron
Dibon
Aroer
Gaza
Hormah?
Arnon
Arad
MOAB
Ar?
Beer-sheba
Sharuhen
Kir-hareseth
Zered
Iye-abarim
Wilderness of Zin
River of Egypt
Punon
Oboth?
Kadesh-barnea
Zalmonah
EDOM
Makheloth
Hor-haggidgad
Rissah
Jotbathah
Wilderness of Paran
Sinai Peninsula
Abronah
Elath
Ezion-geber
Rithmah?
Gulf of Aqaba
Hazeroth?
Alush?
Wilderness of Sinai
Rephidim?
Mt. Sinai
Horeb
7497 ft.
RED SEA
COPYRIGHT. GEORGE PHILIP & SON, LTD.

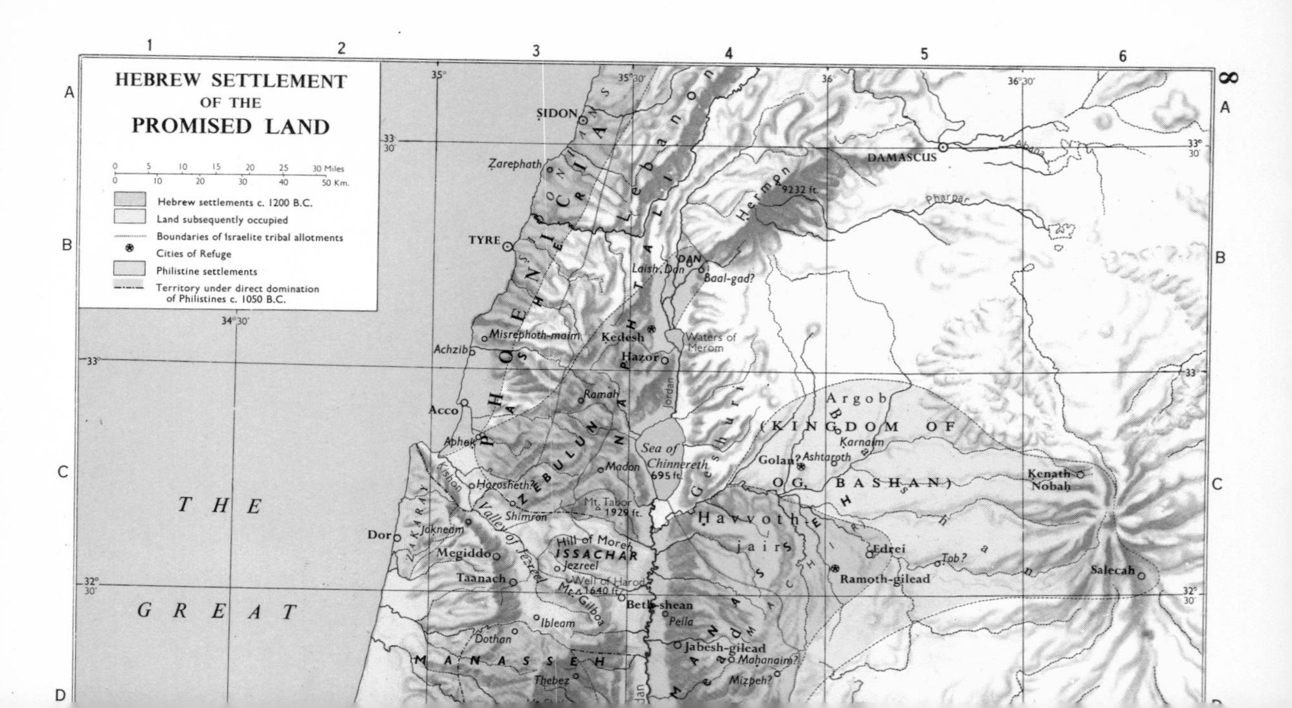
8
HEBREW SETTLEMENT
OF THE
PROMISED LAND
0 5 10 15 20 25 30 Miles
0 10 20 30 40 50 Km.
Hebrew settlements c. 1200 B.C.
Land subsequently occupied
Boundaries of Israelite tribal allotments
Cities of Refuge
Philistine settlements
Territory under direct domination of Philistines c. 1050 B.C.
THE GREAT
SIDON
Zarephath
TYRE
Misrephoth-maim
Achzib
Acco
Aphek
Kishon
Dor
Jokneam
Megiddo
Taanach
Dothan
Ibleam
Thebez
MANASSEH
ISSACHAR
Hill of Moreh
Jezreel
Well of Harod
Mt. Gilboa 1640 ft.
Valley of Jezreel
Shimron
Harosheth
Madon
Mt. Tabor 1929 ft.
ZEBULUN
Ramah
Kedesh
Hazor
Laish, Dan
DAN
Baal-gad?
Waters of Merom
Jordan
Sea of Chinnereth 695 ft.
Beth-shean
Pella
Jabesh-gilead
Mahanaim?
Mizpeh?
Lebanon
Hermon 9232 ft.
DAMASCUS
Abana
Pharpar
Argob
(KINGDOM OF OG, BASHAN)
Karnaim
Ashtaroth
Golan?
Havvoth jairs
Edrei
Ramoth-gilead
Tob?
Kenath Nobah
Salecah
Geshuri
ZAKARAY

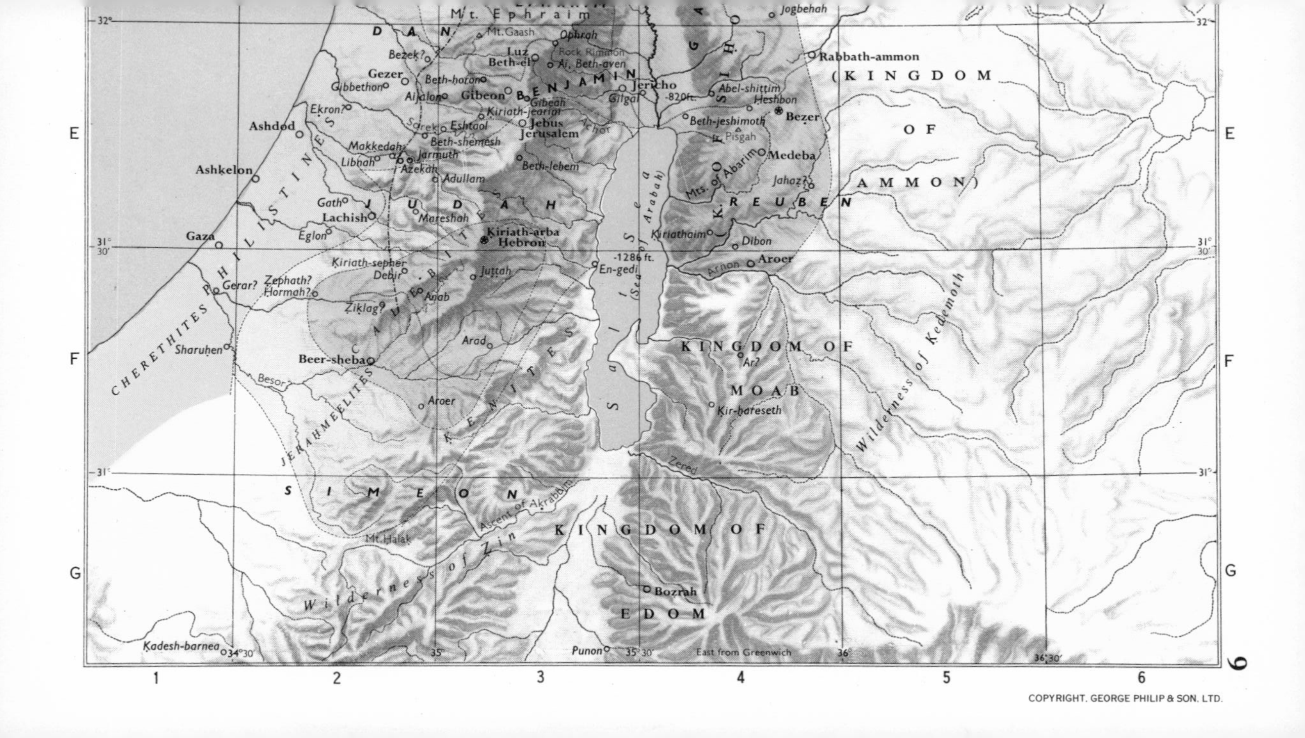

Mt. Ephraim
DAN
Mt. Gaash
Ophrah
Jogbehah
Bezek?
Luz
Beth-el
Rock Rimmon
Ai, Beth-aven
Rabbath-ammon
(KINGDOM OF AMMON)
Gezer
Gibbethon
Beth-horon
Aijalon
Gibeon
BENJAMIN
Jericho
Gilgal
-820 ft.
Abel-shittim
Heshbon
Bezer
Ekron?
Kiriath-jearim
Gibeah
Ashdod
Sorek
Eshtaol
Jebus
Jerusalem
Achor
Beth-jeshimoth
Pisgah
Beth-shemesh
Makkedah
Jarmuth
Libnah
Azekah
Beth-lehem
Abarim
Medeba
Ashkelon
Adullam
Mts.
Jahaz
PHILISTINES
JUDAH
REUBEN
Gath
Lachish
Mareshah
Gaza
Eglon
Kiriath-arba
Hebron
Kiriathaim
Dibon
Aroer
Arnon
-1286 ft.
En-gedi
Salt Sea
(Sea of Arabah)
Kiriath-sepher
Debir
Juttah
Gerar?
Zephath?
Hormah?
Anab
Ziklag?
CALEBITES
Arad
CHERETHITES
Sharuhen
Beer-sheba
KINGDOM OF MOAB
Ar?
Besor
KENITES
JERAHMEELITES
Aroer
Kir-hareseth
Wilderness of Kedemoth
Zered
SIMEON
Ascent of Akrabbim
KINGDOM OF EDOM
Mt. Halak
Wilderness of Zin
Bozrah
Kadesh-barnea
Punon
East from Greenwich
32°
31° 30′
31°
34° 30′
35°
35° 30′
36°
36° 30′
E
F
G
1
2
3
4
5
6
9

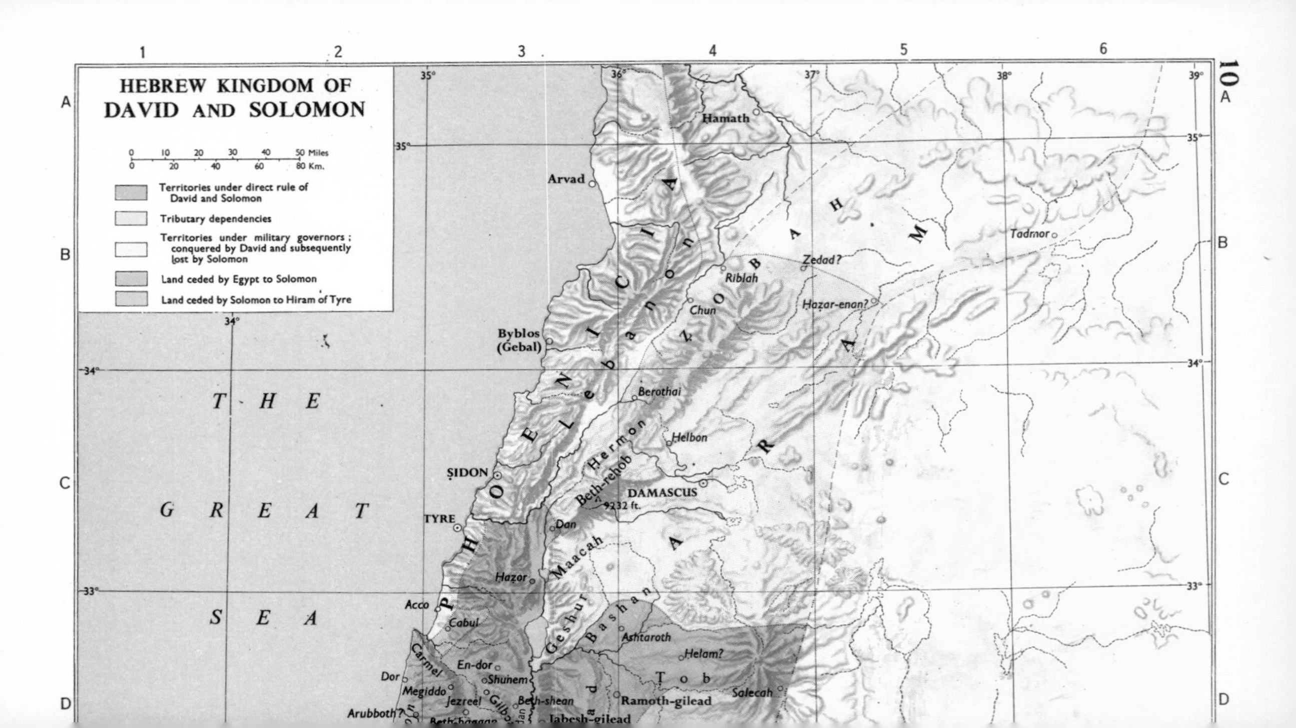
10
HEBREW KINGDOM OF
DAVID AND SOLOMON
0 10 20 30 40 50 Miles
0 20 40 60 80 Km.
Territories under direct rule of David and Solomon
Tributary dependencies
Territories under military governors; conquered by David and subsequently lost by Solomon
Land ceded by Egypt to Solomon
Land ceded by Solomon to Hiram of Tyre
THE GREAT SEA
PHOENICIA
ZOBAH
HAMATH
ARAM
Lebanon
Hermon
Hamath
Arvad
Tadmor
Zedad?
Riblah
Chun
Hazar-enan?
Byblos
(Gebal)
Berothai
Helbon
SIDON
DAMASCUS
Beth-rehob
9232 ft.
TYRE
Dan
Maacah
Hazor
Acco
Cabul
Geshur
Bashan
Ashtaroth
Helam?
Tob
Carmel
En-dor
Shunem
Dor
Megiddo
Jezreel
Gilboa
Beth-shean
Ramoth-gilead
Salecah
Arubboth?
Jabesh-gilead

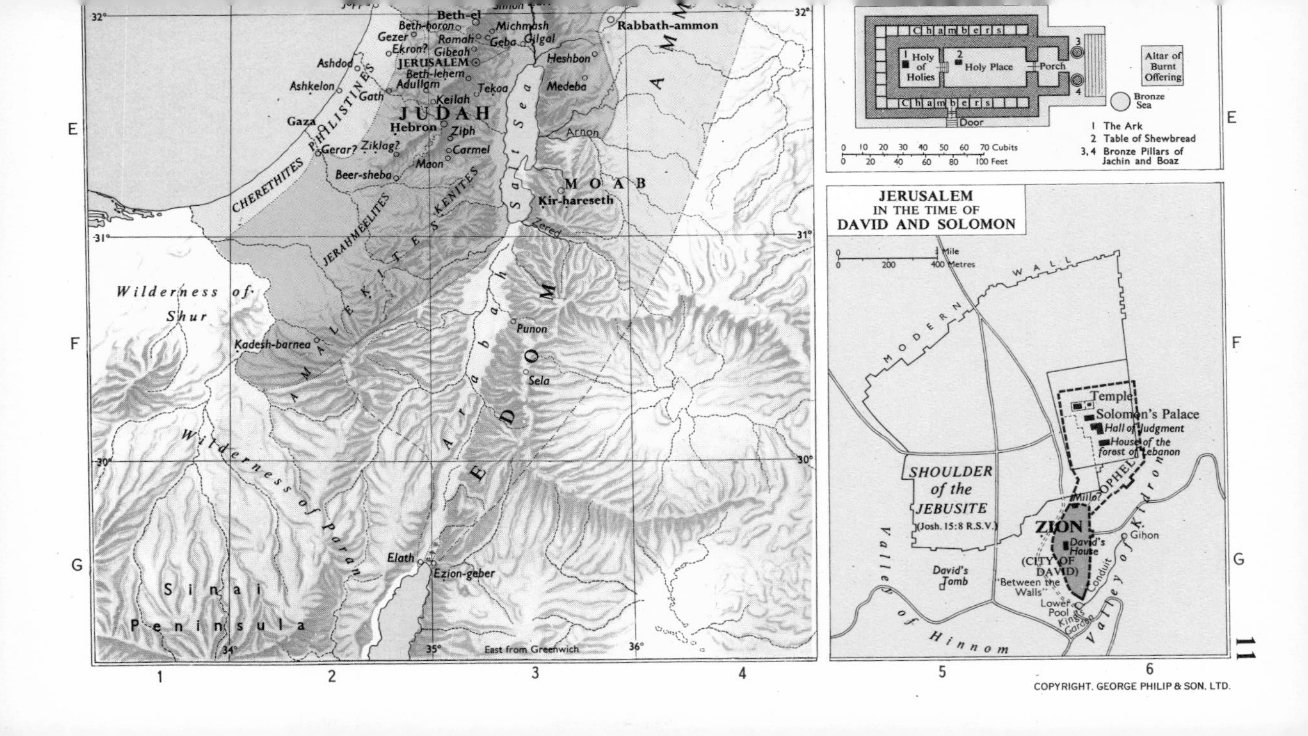

Beth-el
Beth-horon
Michmash
Gezer
Ramah
Geba
Gilgal
Ekron?
Gibeah
JERUSALEM
Beth-lehem
Adullam
Ashdod
Ashkelon
Gath
Tekoa
Keilah
Gaza
PHILISTINES
JUDAH
Hebron
Ziph
Gerar?
Ziklag?
Carmel
Maon
Beer-sheba
CHERETHITES
JERAHMEELITES
KENITES
AMALEKITES
Salt Sea
Rabbath-ammon
AMMON
Heshbon
Medeba
Arnon
MOAB
Kir-hareseth
Zered
Wilderness of Shur
Kadesh-barnea
Arabah
Punon
Sela
EDOM
Wilderness of Paran
Elath
Ezion-geber
Sinai Peninsula
East from Greenwich
32°
31°
30°
34°
35°
36°
1
2
3
4
5
6
E
F
G
Chambers
Holy of Holies
Holy Place
Porch
Door
Altar of Burnt Offering
Bronze Sea
1 The Ark
2 Table of Shewbread
3, 4 Bronze Pillars of Jachin and Boaz
0 10 20 30 40 50 60 70 Cubits
0 20 40 60 80 100 Feet
JERUSALEM
IN THE TIME OF
DAVID AND SOLOMON
0 Mile
0 200 400 Metres
MODERN WALL
Temple
Solomon's Palace
Hall of Judgment
House of the forest of Lebanon
OPHEL
Millo?
SHOULDER of the JEBUSITE
(Josh. 15:8 R.S.V.)
ZION
David's House
(CITY OF DAVID)
Gihon
Valley of Kidron
Conduit
David's Tomb
"Between the Walls"
Lower Pool
King's Garden
Valley of Hinnom

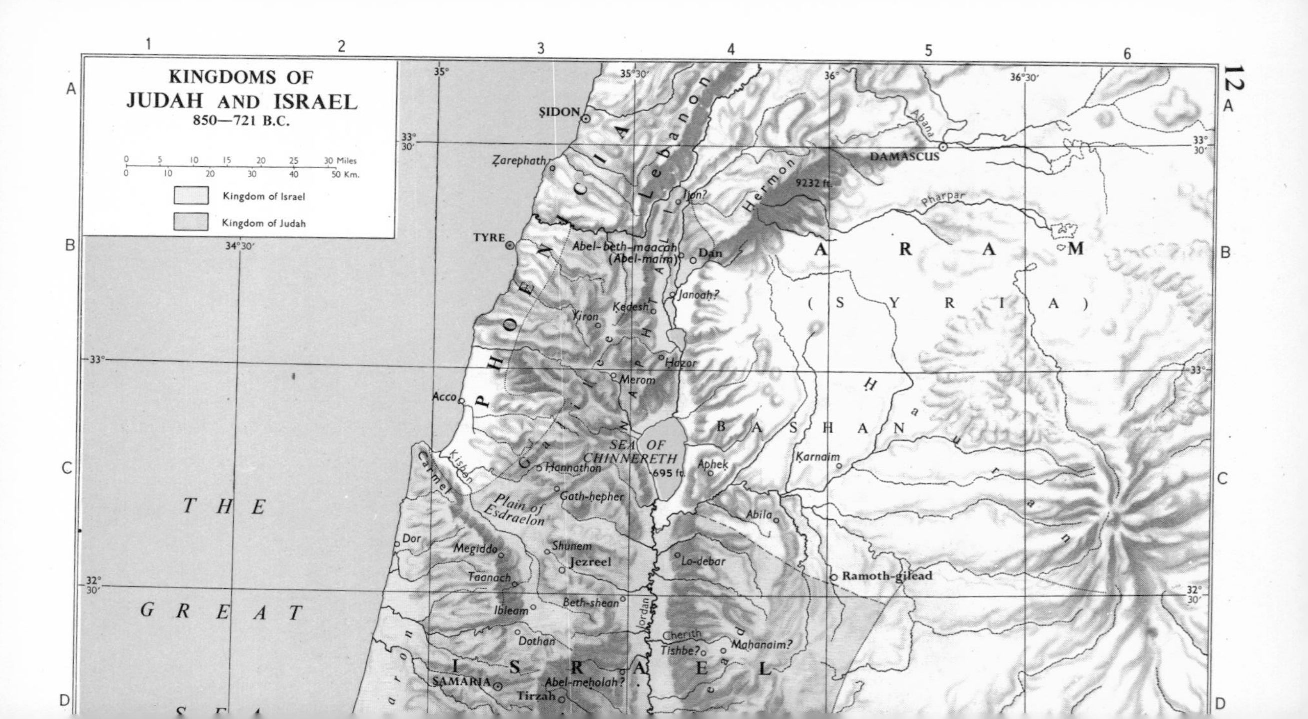
12
KINGDOMS OF JUDAH AND ISRAEL
850—721 B.C.
0 5 10 15 20 25 30 Miles
0 10 20 30 40 50 Km.
Kingdom of Israel
Kingdom of Judah
ṢIDON
Ẓarephath
TYRE
Acco
PHOENICIA
Lebanon
Ijon?
Hermon
9232 ft.
DAMASCUS
Abana
Pharpar
ARAM
(SYRIA)
Abel-beth-maacah
(Abel-maim)
Dan
Janoah?
Ḳedesh
Yiron
Hazor
Merom
NAPHTALI
Galilee
SEA OF CHINNERETH
695 ft.
Hannathon
Gath-hepher
Plain of Esdraelon
Kishon
Carmel
Aphek
Karnaim
BASHAN
Ḥauran
Abila
Lo-debar
Ramoth-gilead
Dor
Megiddo
Shunem
Jezreel
Taanach
Ibleam
Beth-shean
Jordan
Dothan
Cherith
Tishbe?
Mahanaim?
ISRAEL
SAMARIA
Abel-meholah?
Tirzah
THE GREAT SEA
35°
35°30′
36°
36°30′
34°30′
33°
32° 30′

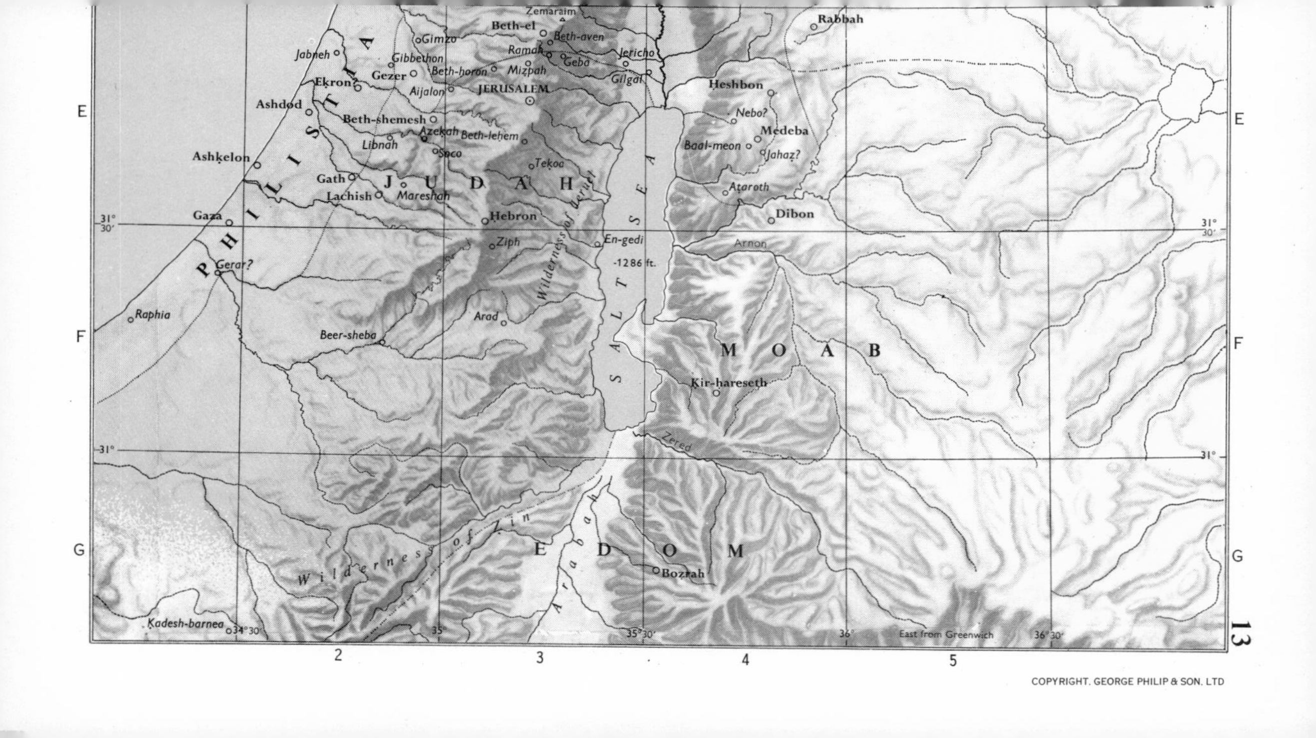
Rabbah
Zemaraim
Beth-el
Beth-aven
Gimzo
Jabneh
Gibbethon
Ramah
Geba
Jericho
Gezer
Beth-horon
Mizpah
Gilgal
Ekron?
Aijalon
JERUSALEM
Heshbon
Ashdod
Beth-shemesh
Nebo?
Medeba
Azekah
Beth-lehem
Libnah
Baal-meon
Jahaz?
Soco
Ashkelon
Tekoa
Gath
JUDAH
Ataroth
Lachish
Mareshah
Dibon
Gaza
Hebron
PHILISTIA
SALT SEA
En-gedi
Ziph
Arnon
-1286 ft.
Gerar?
Wilderness of Judah
Raphia
Arad
Beer-sheba
MOAB
Kir-hareseth
Zered
Wilderness of Zin
Arabah
EDOM
Bozrah
Kadesh-barnea
31° 30′
31°
34° 30′
35°
35° 30′
36°
36° 30′
East from Greenwich
E
F
G
2
3
4
5

(BLACK SEA)
HELLAS
Athens
Argos
Sparta
Troy
LYDIA
Sardis
(Sepharad)
CARIANS
PHRYGIA
Halys
Pteria
Hattushash
Kanish
Taurus
Tarsus
CAPHTOR
KITTIM
Alalakh
Ugarit
THE GREAT SEA
Arvad
Byblos
(Gebal)
Sidon
Tyre
PHOENICIA
Megiddo
Samaria
Lachish
Gaza
PHILISTIA
JUDAH
Jordan
AMMON
Jerusalem
MOAB
EDOM
Sais
Tahpanhes
On
MEMPHIS
(Noph)
Elath
Sinai
Nile
EGYPT
Thebes
(No)
East from 35° Greenwich

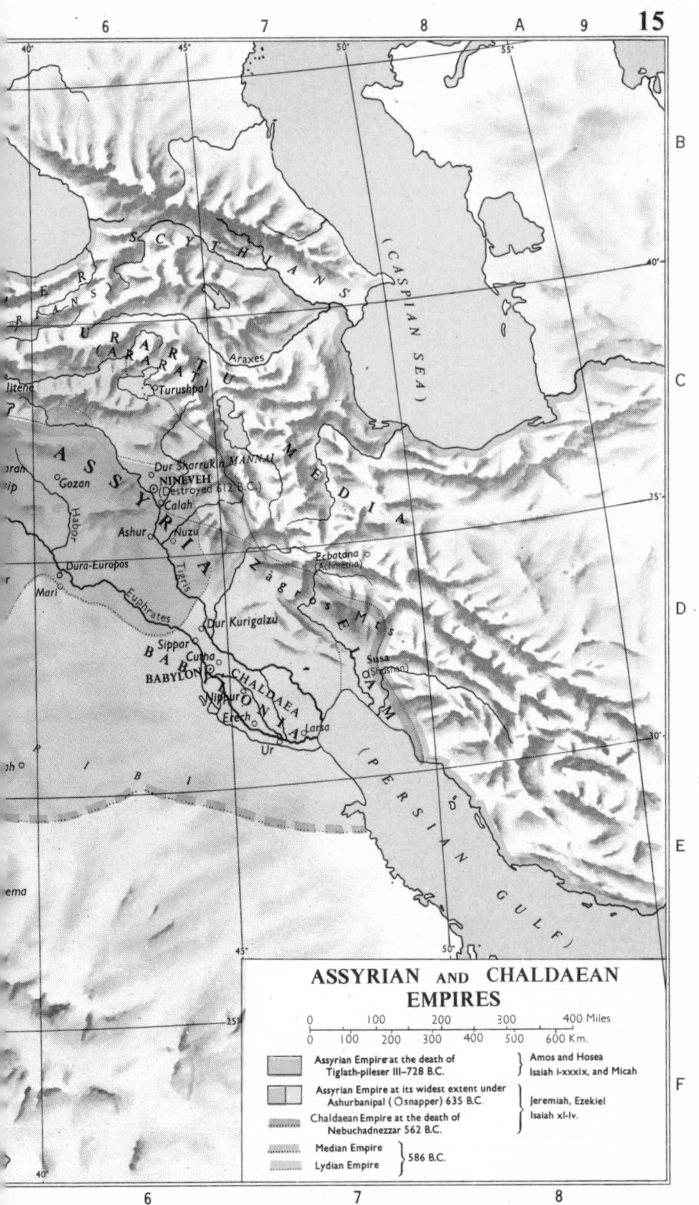
6
7
8
A
9
B
C
D
E
F
40°
45°
50°
55°
35°
30°
25°
SCYTHIANS
(CASPIAN SEA)
URARTU
(ARARAT)
Araxes
Turushpa
Litene
MANNAI
MEDIA
ASSYRIA
Dur Sharrukin
NINEVEH
(Destroyed 612 B.C.)
Calah
Gozan
Habor
Ashur
Nuzu
Tigris
Dura-Europos
Mari
Euphrates
Ecbatana
(Achmetha)
Zagros Mts.
Dur Kurigalzu
Sippar
Cutha
BABYLON
BABYLONIA
CHALDAEA
Nippur
Erech
Larsa
Ur
Susa
(Shushan)
ELAM
(PERSIAN GULF)
ASSYRIAN AND CHALDAEAN EMPIRES
0 100 200 300 400 Miles
0 100 200 300 400 500 600 Km.
Assyrian Empire at the death of Tiglath-pileser III–728 B.C.
Amos and Hosea
Isaiah i-xxxix, and Micah
Assyrian Empire at its widest extent under Ashurbanipal (Osnapper) 635 B.C.
Chaldaean Empire at the death of Nebuchadnezzar 562 B.C.
Jeremiah, Ezekiel
Isaiah xl-lv.
Median Empire
Lydian Empire
586 B.C.
6
7
8

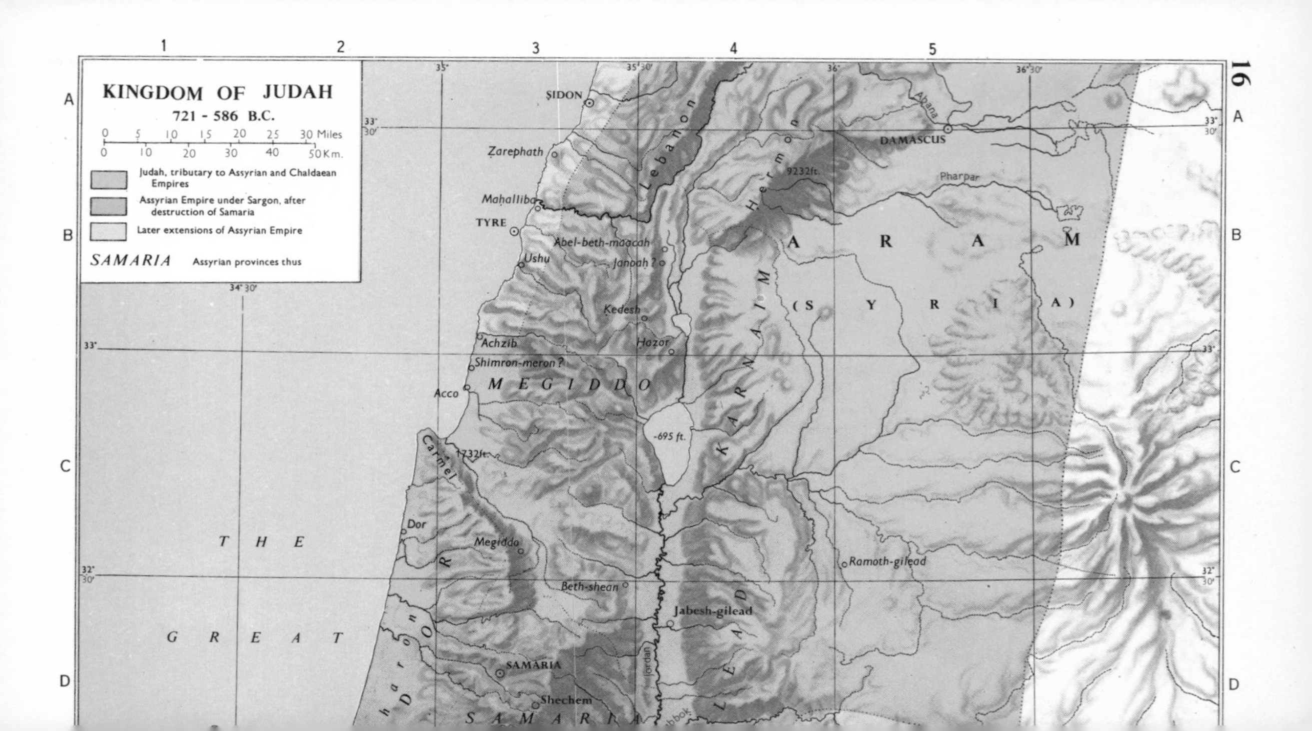
KINGDOM OF JUDAH
721 - 586 B.C.
0 5 10 15 20 25 30 Miles
0 10 20 30 40 50 Km.
Judah, tributary to Assyrian and Chaldaean Empires
Assyrian Empire under Sargon, after destruction of Samaria
Later extensions of Assyrian Empire
SAMARIA Assyrian provinces thus
SIDON
Zarephath
Lebanon
Hermon
9232 ft.
Abana
DAMASCUS
Pharpar
Mahalliba
TYRE
Abel-beth-maacah
Janoah ?
Ushu
ARAM
(SYRIA)
KARNAIM
Kedesh
Achzib
Hazor
Shimron-meron ?
MEGIDDO
Acco
-695 ft.
Carmel
1732 ft.
Dor
THE
Megiddo
Ramoth-gilead
Beth-shean
Jabesh-gilead
GILEAD
GREAT
SAMARIA
Jordan
Shechem
Jabbok

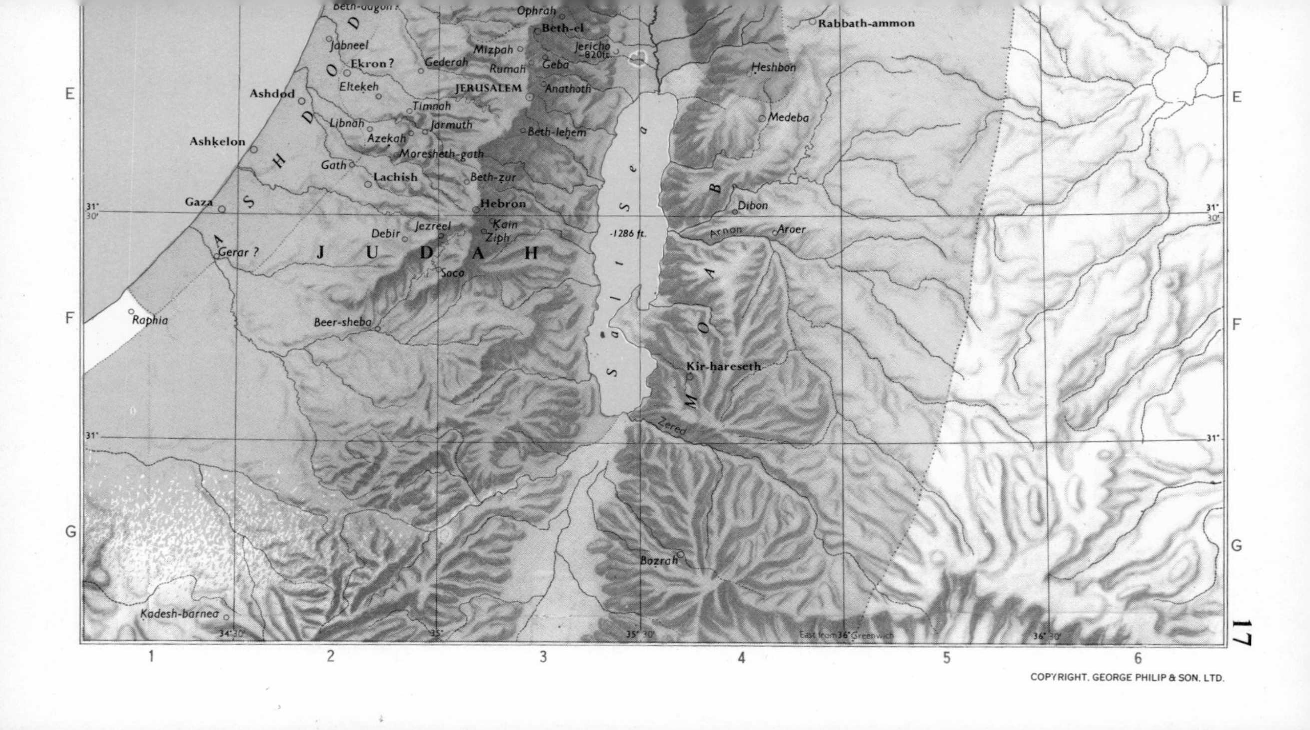
Ophrah
Beth-el
Rabbath-ammon
Jabneel
Mizpah
Jericho
-820ft.
Ekron?
Gederah
Rumah
Geba
Heshbon
Elteḳeh
JERUSALEM
Anathoth
Ashdod
Timnah
Libnah
Jarmuth
Medeba
Beth-leḥem
Azekah
Ashḳelon
Moresheth-gath
Gath
Lachish
Beth-ẓur
Gaza
Hebron
Dibon
Debir
Jezreel
Kain
Ziph
Arnon
Aroer
-1286 ft.
Gerar ?
J U D A H
Soco
Raphia
Beer-sheba
Kir-hareseth
Zered
Bozrah
Kadesh-barnea
34° 30'
35°
35° 30'
East from 36° Greenwich
36° 30'
31° 30'
31°
E
F
G
1
2
3
4
5
6

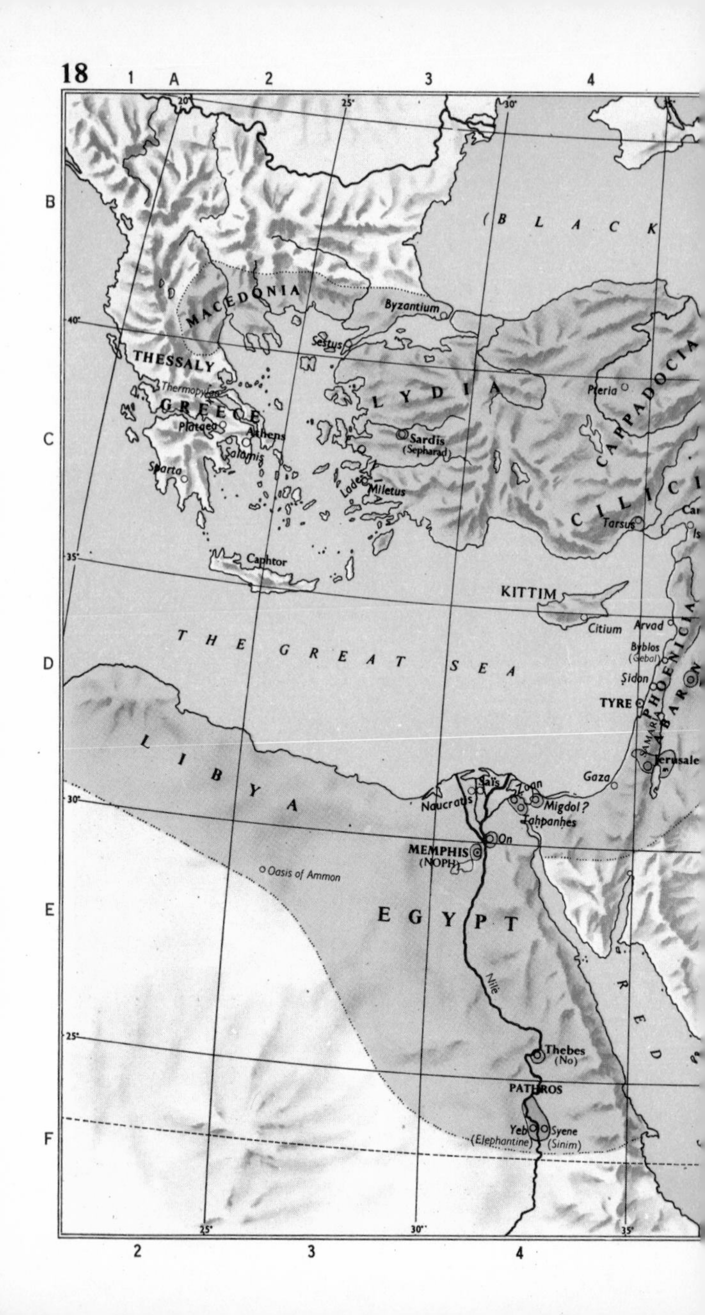

BLACK
MACEDONIA
Byzantium
Sestus
THESSALY
Thermopylae
GREECE
Plataea
Athens
Salamis
Sparta
LYDIA
Sardis
(Sepharad)
Lade
Miletus
Pteria
CAPPADOCIA
CILICI
Tarsus
Caphtor
KITTIM
Citium
Arvad
Byblos
(Gebal)
Sidon
TYRE
PHOENICIA
SAMARIA
Jerusale
THE GREAT SEA
LIBYA
Gaza
Saïs
Zoan
Naucratis
Migdol?
Tahpanhes
On
MEMPHIS
(NOPH)
Oasis of Ammon
EGYPT
Nile
RED
Thebes
(No)
PATHROS
Yeb
(Elephantine)
Syene
(Sinim)

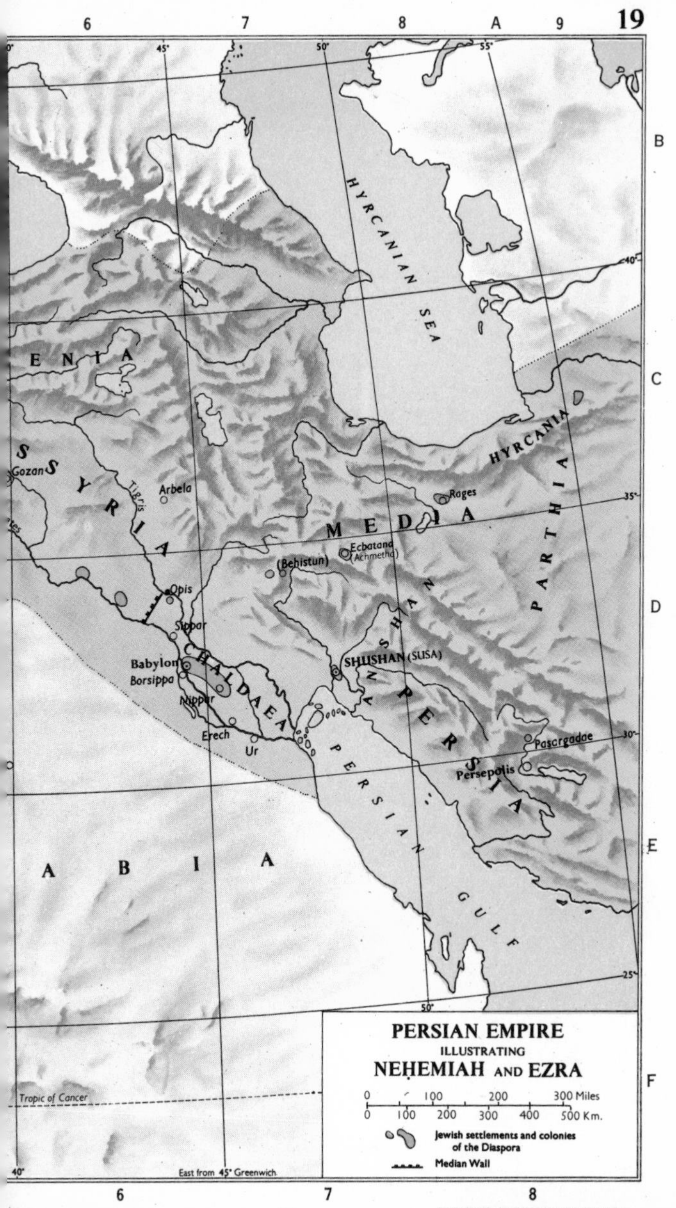

HYRCANIAN SEA
HYRCANIA
PARTHIA
MEDIA
Rages
Ecbatana
(Achmetha)
(Behistun)
Arbela
Gozan
SYRIA
Tigris
Opis
Sippar
CHALDAEA
Babylon
Borsippa
Nippur
Erech
Ur
SHUSHAN (SUSA)
SHUSHAN
PERSIA
Pasargadae
Persepolis
PERSIAN GULF
ENIA
ABIA
Tropic of Cancer
East from 45° Greenwich
PERSIAN EMPIRE
ILLUSTRATING
NEHEMIAH AND EZRA
0 100 200 300 Miles
0 100 200 300 400 500 Km.
Jewish settlements and colonies of the Diaspora
Median Wall

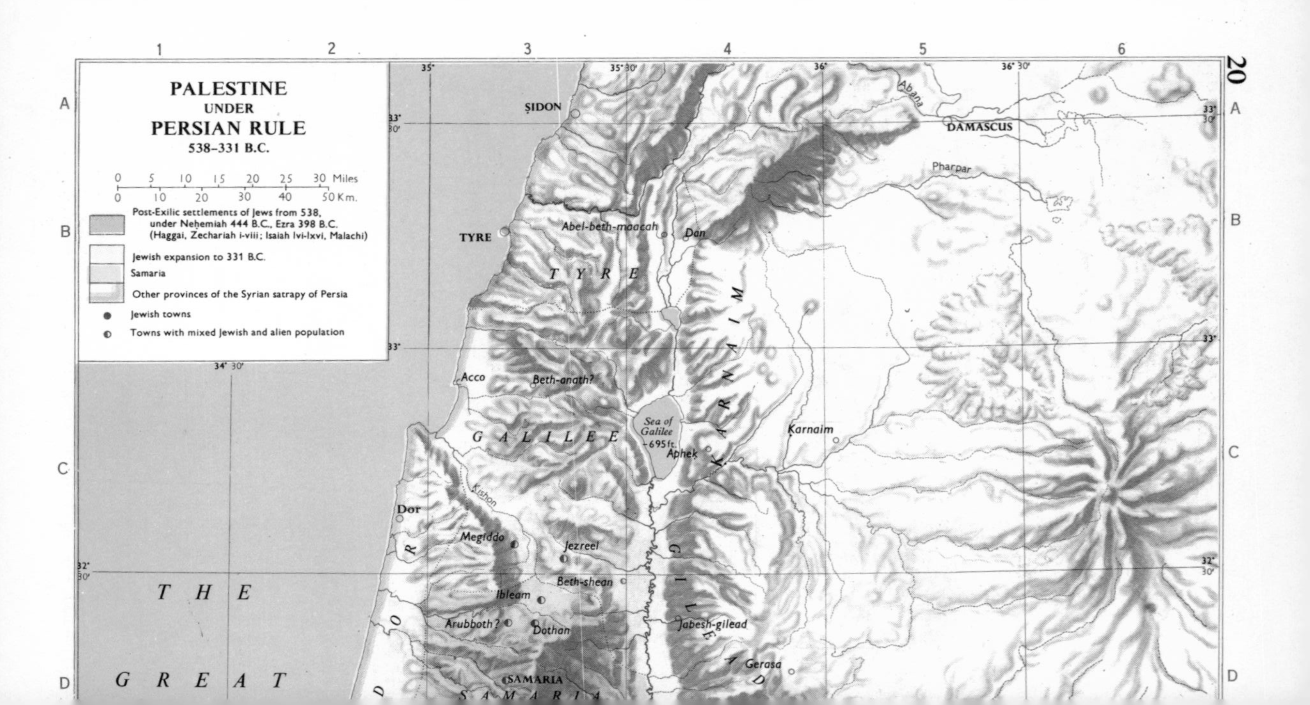
PALESTINE
UNDER
PERSIAN RULE
538–331 B.C.
0 5 10 15 20 25 30 Miles
0 10 20 30 40 50 Km.
Post-Exilic settlements of Jews from 538, under Nehemiah 444 B.C., Ezra 398 B.C. (Haggai, Zechariah i-viii; Isaiah lvi-lxvi, Malachi)
Jewish expansion to 331 B.C.
Samaria
Other provinces of the Syrian satrapy of Persia
Jewish towns
Towns with mixed Jewish and alien population
SIDON
TYRE
DAMASCUS
Abana
Pharpar
Abel-beth-maacah
Dan
T Y R E
K A R N A I M
Acco
Beth-anath?
G A L I L E E
Sea of Galilee -695 ft.
Aphek
Karnaim
Kishon
Dor
Megiddo
Jezreel
Beth-shean
Ibleam
Arubboth?
Dothan
Jabesh-gilead
Gerasa
G I L E A D
SAMARIA
THE GREAT

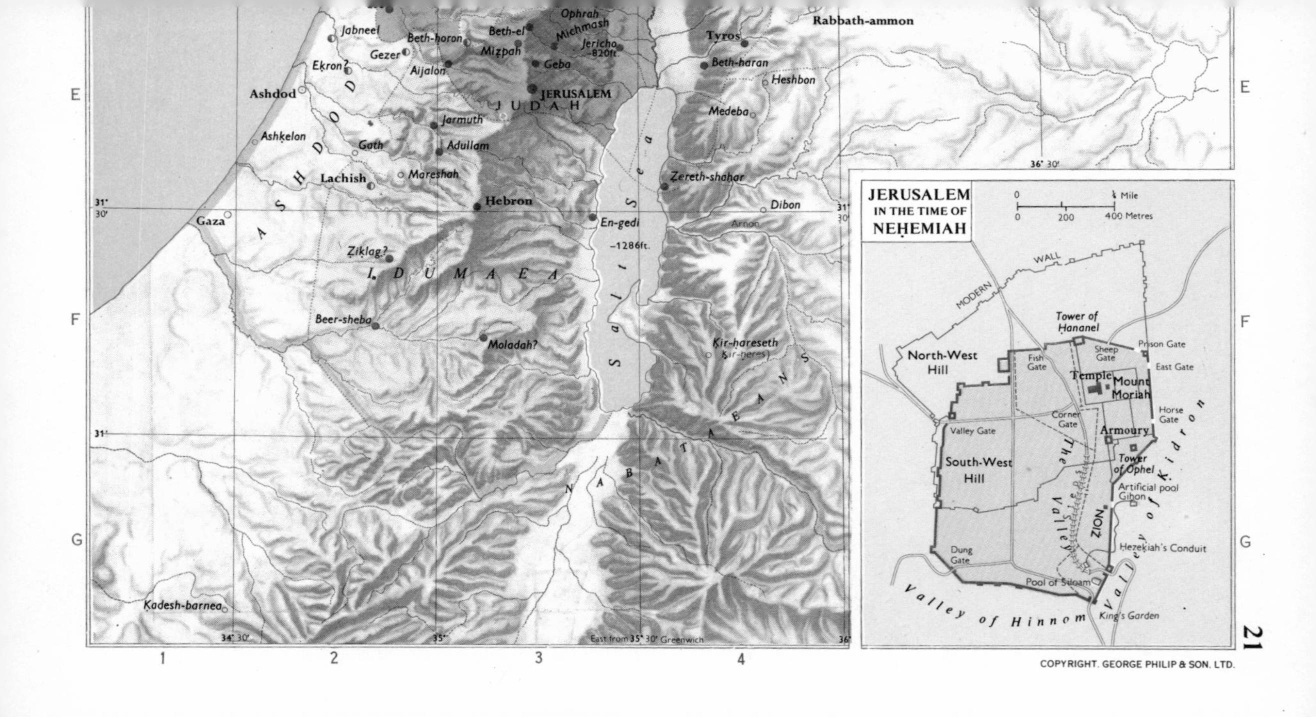

Rabbath-ammon
Jabneel
Beth-horon
Beth-el
Ophrah
Michmash
Jericho
-820ft.
Tyros
Gezer
Mizpah
Ekron?
Aijalon
Geba
Beth-haran
Heshbon
Ashdod
JERUSALEM
JUDAH
Medeba
Jarmuth
Ashkelon
Gath
Adullam
ASHDOD
Lachish
Mareshah
Zereth-shahar
Hebron
Dibon
Gaza
En-gedi
Arnon
-1286ft.
Salt Sea
Ziklag?
IDUMAEA
Beer-sheba
Moladah?
Kir-hareseth
(Kir-heres)
NABATAEANS
Kadesh-barnea
31° 30'
31°
34° 30'
35°
East from 35° 30' Greenwich
36°
36° 30'
E
F
G
1
2
3
4
JERUSALEM
IN THE TIME OF
NEHEMIAH
0
¼ Mile
0
200
400 Metres
MODERN WALL
Tower of Hananel
North-West Hill
Fish Gate
Sheep Gate
Prison Gate
East Gate
Temple
Mount Moriah
Corner Gate
Horse Gate
Valley Gate
Armoury
South-West Hill
The Valley
Tower of Ophel
Artificial pool
Gihon
ZION
Valley of Kidron
Dung Gate
Hezekiah's Conduit
Pool of Siloam
Valley of Hinnom
King's Garden

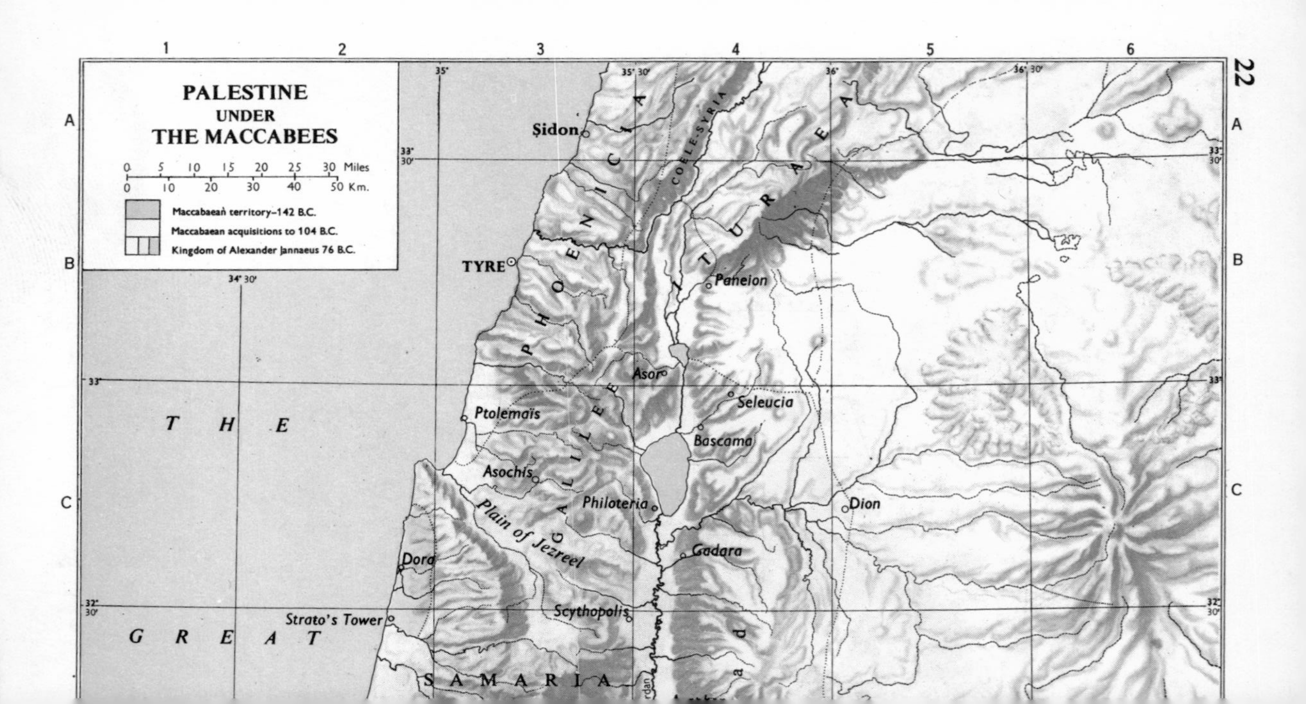
PALESTINE
UNDER
THE MACCABEES
0 5 10 15 20 25 30 Miles
0 10 20 30 40 50 Km.
Maccabaean territory–142 B.C.
Maccabaean acquisitions to 104 B.C.
Kingdom of Alexander Jannaeus 76 B.C.
PHOENICIA
COELE-SYRIA
ITURAEA
GALILEE
SAMARIA
THE GREAT
Ṣidon
TYRE
Paneion
Asor
Seleucia
Bascama
Ptolemais
Asochis
Philoteria
Dion
Plain of Jezreel
Gadara
Dora
Scythopolis
Strato's Tower

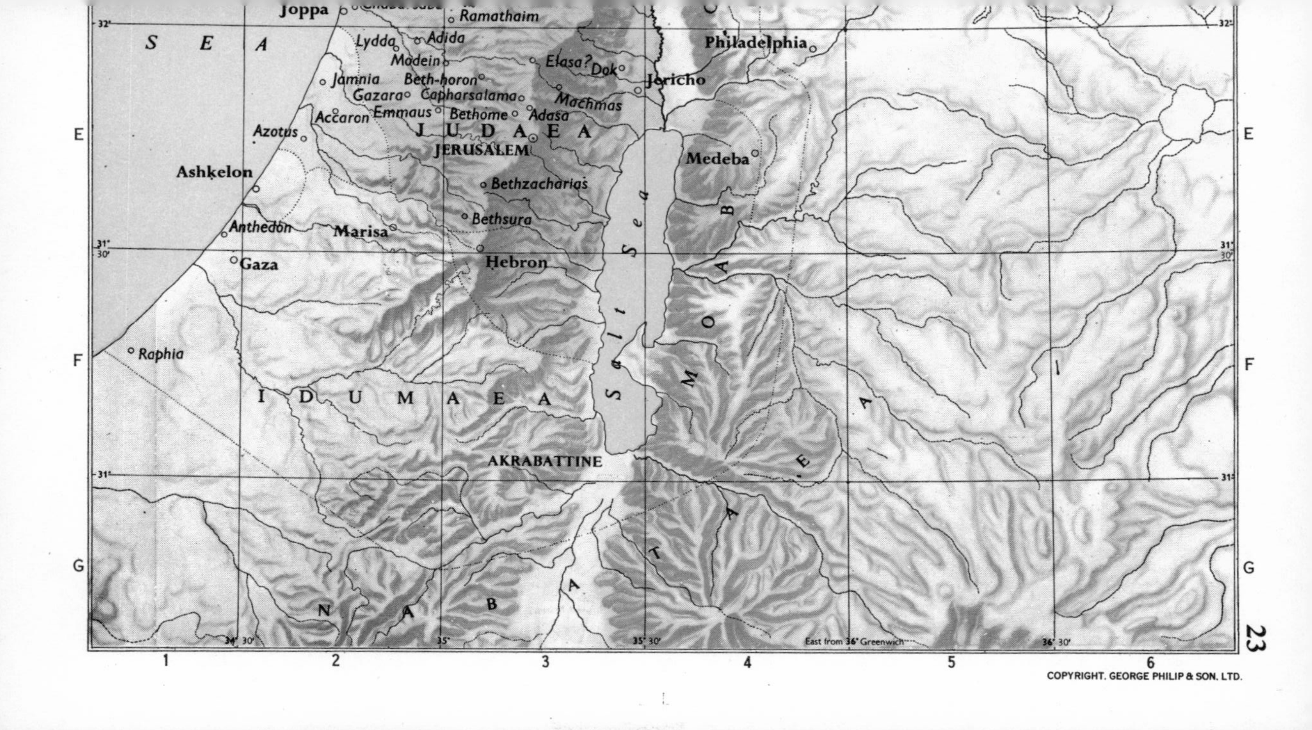
Joppa
Ramathaim
SEA
Lydda
Adida
Modein
Elasa?
Dok
Jamnia
Beth-horon
Jericho
Philadelphia
Gazara
Capharsalama
Machmas
Accaron
Emmaus
Bethome
Adasa
Azotus
JUDAEA
JERUSALEM
Medeba
Ashkelon
Bethzacharias
Bethsura
Anthedon
Marisa
Gaza
Hebron
Salt Sea
MOAB
Raphia
IDUMAEA
AKRABATTINE
NABATAEA
32°
31° 30′
31°
34° 30′
35°
35° 30′
East from 36° Greenwich
36° 30′
E
F
G
1
2
3
4
5
6

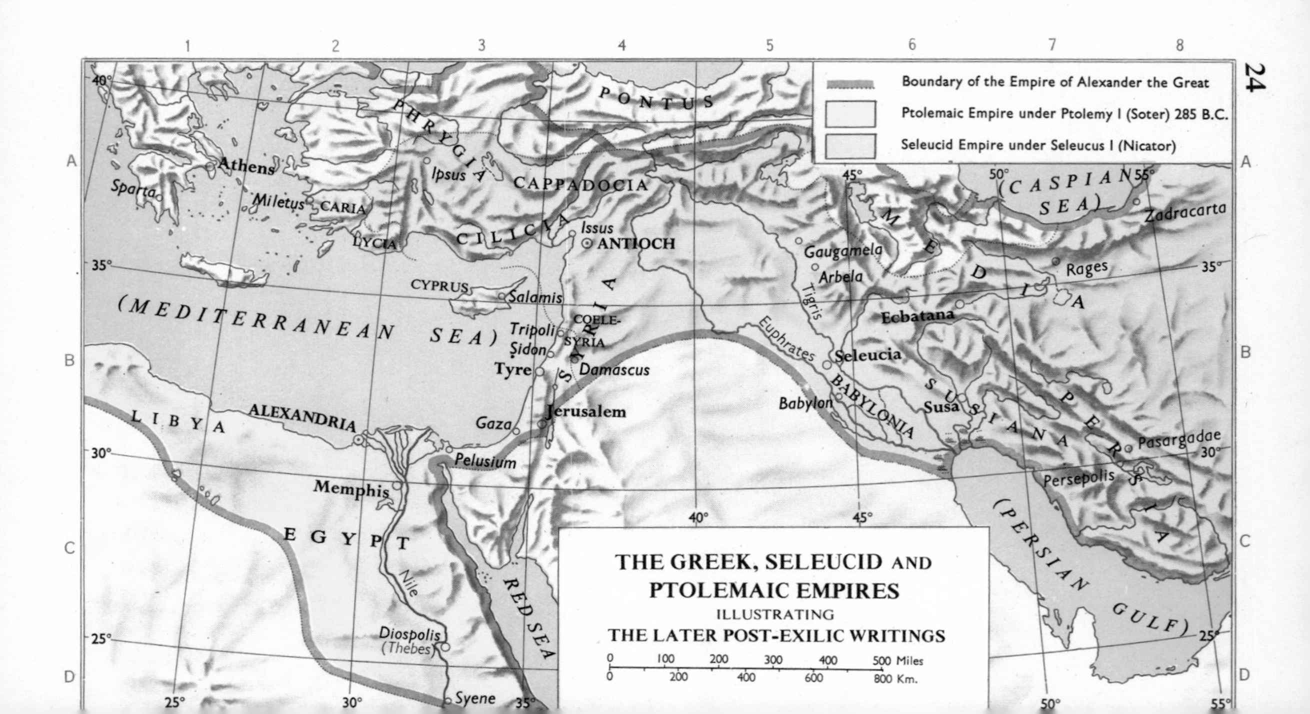
THE GREEK, SELEUCID AND PTOLEMAIC EMPIRES
ILLUSTRATING
THE LATER POST-EXILIC WRITINGS
Boundary of the Empire of Alexander the Great
Ptolemaic Empire under Ptolemy I (Soter) 285 B.C.
Seleucid Empire under Seleucus I (Nicator)
0 100 200 300 400 500 Miles
0 200 400 600 800 Km.
PONTUS
PHRYGIA
Ipsus
CAPPADOCIA
CILICIA
Issus
ANTIOCH
Athens
Sparta
Miletus
CARIA
LYCIA
CYPRUS
Salamis
(MEDITERRANEAN SEA)
Tripoli
Sidon
Tyre
COELE-SYRIA
SYRIA
Damascus
Jerusalem
Gaza
Pelusium
LIBYA
ALEXANDRIA
Memphis
EGYPT
Nile
Diospolis (Thebes)
Syene
RED SEA
Gaugamela
Arbela
Tigris
Euphrates
Seleucia
Babylon
BABYLONIA
Ecbatana
MEDIA
Rages
(CASPIAN SEA)
Zadracarta
Susa
SUSIANA
PERSIA
Pasargadae
Persepolis
(PERSIAN GULF)
A
B
C
D
1
2
3
4
5
6
7
8
40°
35°
30°
25°
45°
50°
55°

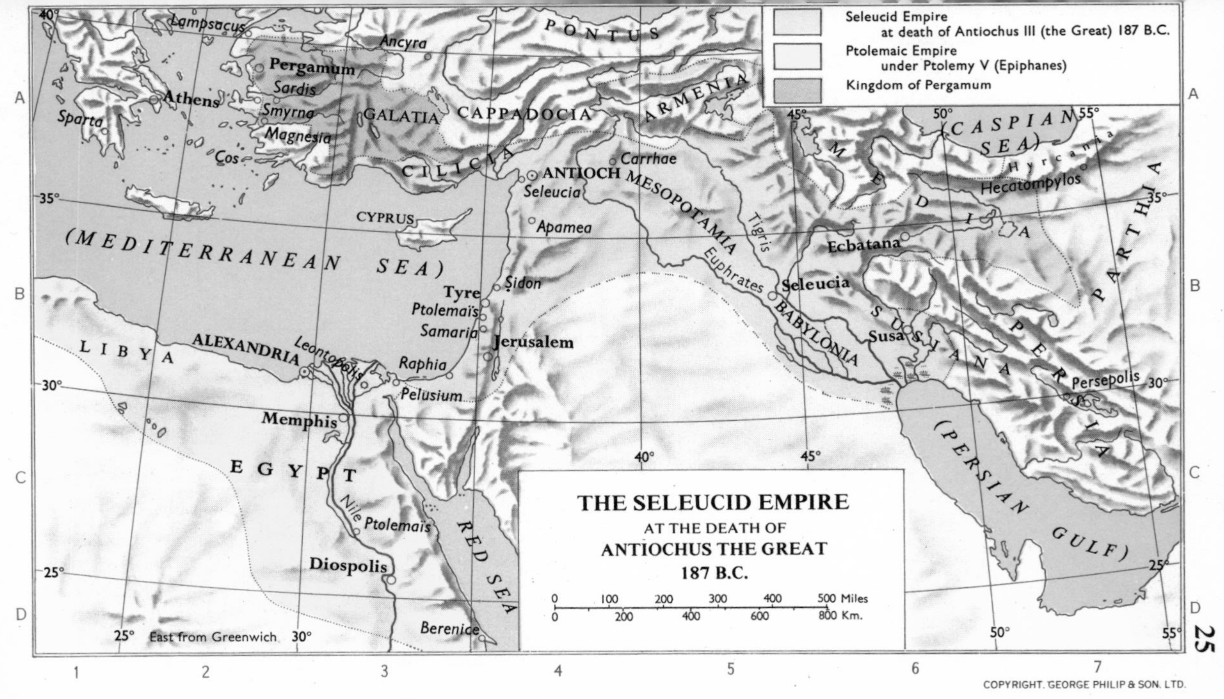
THE SELEUCID EMPIRE
AT THE DEATH OF
ANTIOCHUS THE GREAT
187 B.C.
Seleucid Empire at death of Antiochus III (the Great) 187 B.C.
Ptolemaic Empire under Ptolemy V (Epiphanes)
Kingdom of Pergamum
0 100 200 300 400 500 Miles
0 200 400 600 800 Km.
PONTUS
ARMENIA
CAPPADOCIA
GALATIA
CILICIA
MESOPOTAMIA
MEDIA
PARTHIA
PERSIA
SUSIANA
BABYLONIA
Hyrcania
(CASPIAN SEA)
(MEDITERRANEAN SEA)
(PERSIAN GULF)
RED SEA
LIBYA
EGYPT
CYPRUS
Lampsacus
Ancyra
Pergamum
Sardis
Athens
Smyrna
Sparta
Magnesia
Cos
Carrhae
ANTIOCH
Seleucia
Apamea
Hecatompylos
Ecbatana
Tigris
Euphrates
Seleucia
Sidon
Tyre
Ptolemaïs
Samaria
Jerusalem
Susa
Persepolis
ALEXANDRIA
Leontopolis
Raphia
Pelusium
Memphis
Nile
Ptolemaïs
Diospolis
Berenice
East from Greenwich
COPYRIGHT. GEORGE PHILIP & SON. LTD.

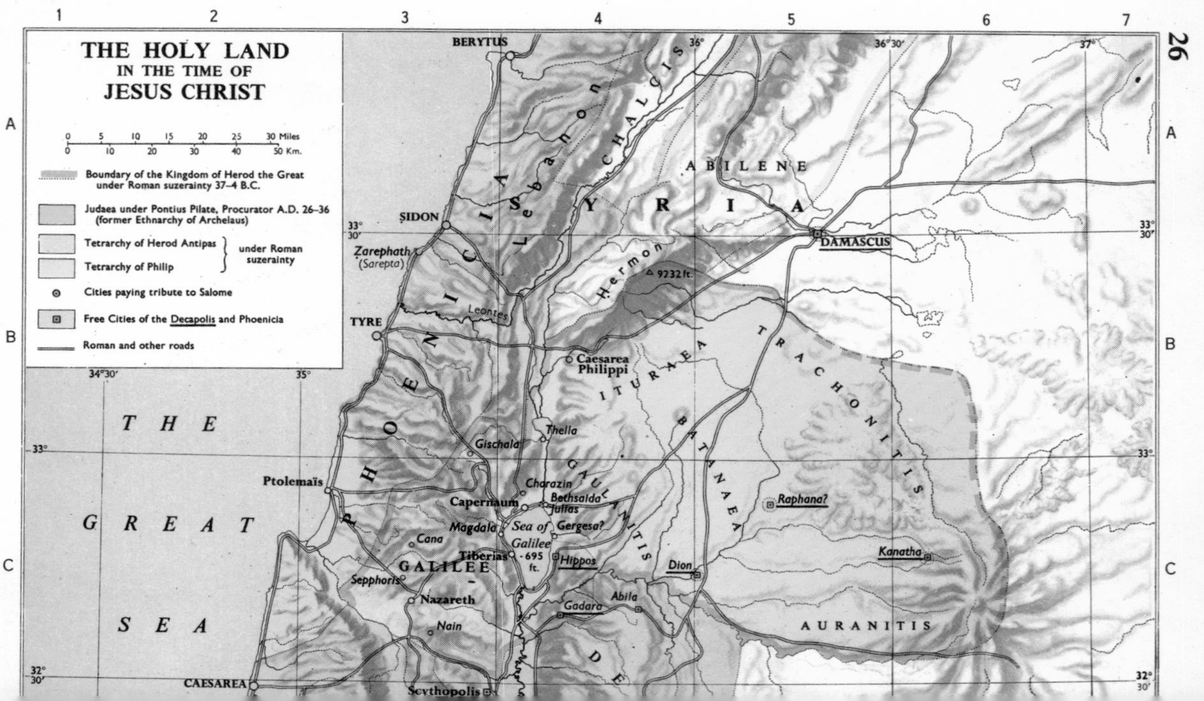
THE HOLY LAND
IN THE TIME OF
JESUS CHRIST
0 5 10 15 20 25 30 Miles
0 10 20 30 40 50 Km.
Boundary of the Kingdom of Herod the Great under Roman suzerainty 37–4 B.C.
Judaea under Pontius Pilate, Procurator A.D. 26–36 (former Ethnarchy of Archelaus)
Tetrarchy of Herod Antipas
Tetrarchy of Philip
under Roman suzerainty
Cities paying tribute to Salome
Free Cities of the Decapolis and Phoenicia
Roman and other roads
THE GREAT SEA
BERYTUS
SIDON
Zarephath (Sarepta)
TYRE
Leontes
Ptolemaïs
CAESAREA
PHOENICIA
Lebanon
CHALCIS
ABILENE
SYRIA
DAMASCUS
Hermon
9232 ft.
Caesarea Philippi
ITURAEA
TRACHONITIS
BATANAEA
GAULANITIS
Thella
Gischala
Chorazin
Capernaum
Bethsaida Julias
Magdala
Sea of Galilee
-695 ft.
Gergesa?
Tiberias
Hippos
GALILEE
Cana
Sepphoris
Nazareth
Nain
Gadara
Abila
Dion
Raphana?
Kanatha
AURANITIS
Scythopolis
DE
1 2 3 4 5 6 7
A B C
34°30′ 35° 36° 36°30′ 37°
33° 33°30′ 32°30′

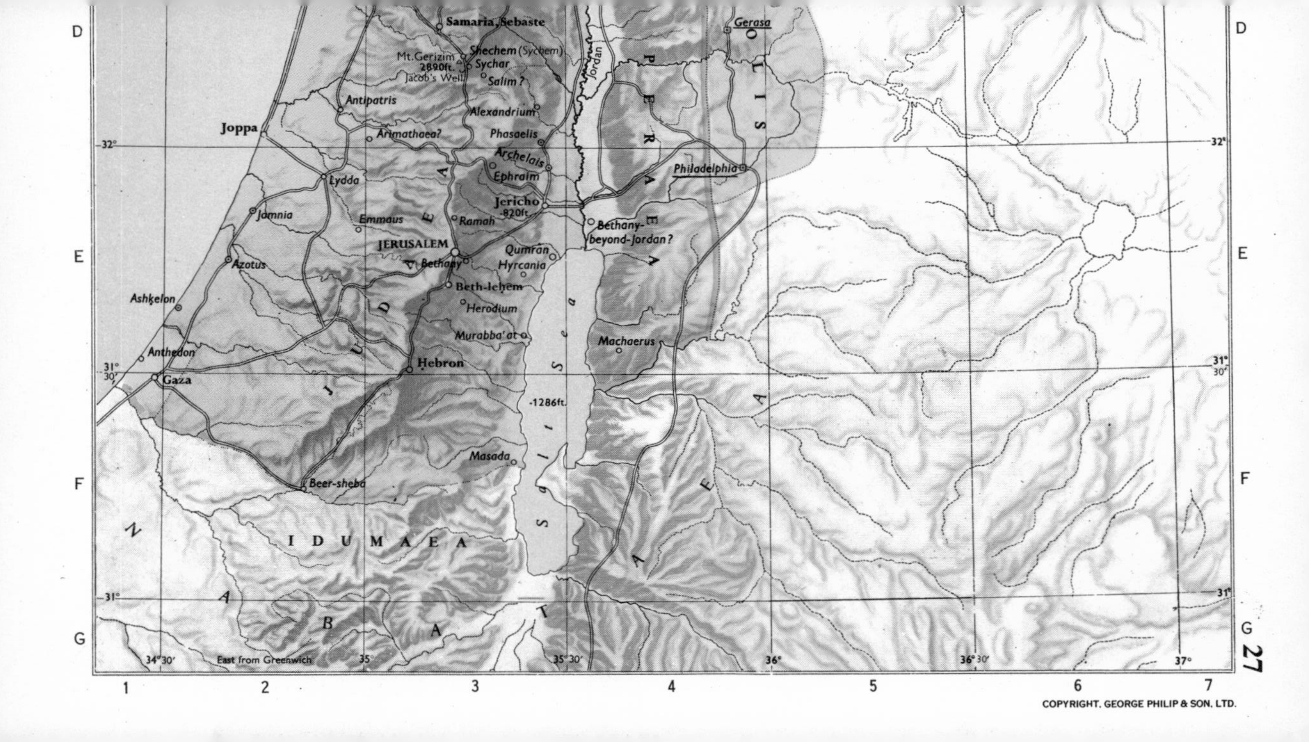
Samaria, Sebaste
Shechem (Sychem)
Mt. Gerizim
2890ft.
Sychar
Jacob's Well
Salim ?
Antipatris
Alexandrium
Joppa
Arimathaea?
Phasaelis
Archelais
Ephraim
Lydda
Jericho
-820ft.
Jamnia
Emmaus
Ramah
JERUSALEM
Bethany
Qumran
Hyrcania
Azotus
Beth-lehem
Herodium
Ashkelon
Murabba'at
Anthedon
Hebron
Gaza
-1286ft.
Masada
Beer-sheba
JUDAEA
IDUMAEA
NABATAEA
PERAEA
Jordan
Gerasa
Philadelphia
Bethany-beyond-Jordan?
Machaerus
Salt Sea
East from Greenwich
34°30'
35°
35°30'
36°
36°30'
37°
32°
31° 30'
31°
D
E
F
G
1
2
3
4
5
6
7

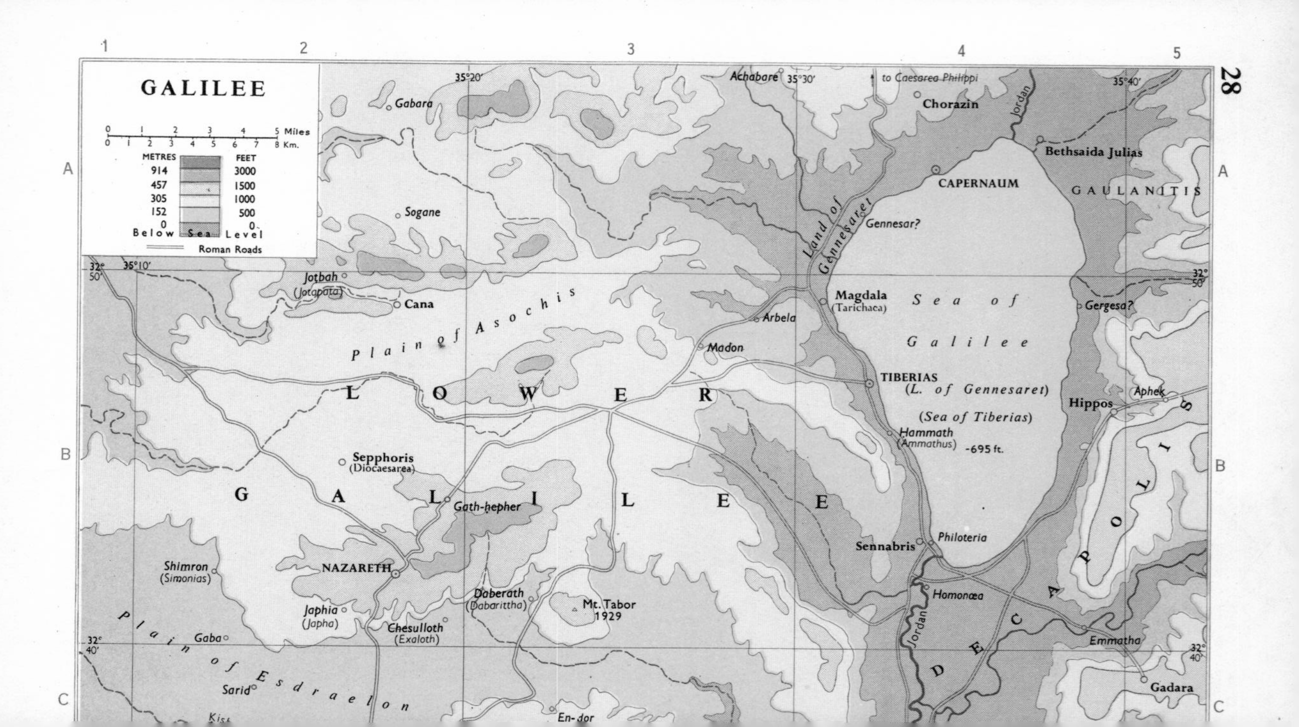
GALILEE
0 1 2 3 4 5 Miles
0 1 2 3 4 5 6 7 8 Km.
METRES FEET
914 3000
457 1500
305 1000
152 500
0 0
Below Sea Level
Roman Roads
35°10′
35°20′
35°30′
35°40′
32° 50′
32° 40′
Gabara
Sogane
Jotbah
(Jotapata)
Cana
Plain of Asochis
Achabare
to Caesarea Philippi
Chorazin
Jordan
Bethsaida Julias
CAPERNAUM
GAULANITIS
Land of Gennesaret
Gennesar?
Magdala
(Tarichaea)
Sea of Galilee
Gergesa?
Arbela
Madon
TIBERIAS
(L. of Gennesaret)
(Sea of Tiberias)
Hammath
(Ammathus)
-695 ft.
Hippos
Aphek
LOWER GALILEE
DECAPOLIS
Sepphoris
(Diocaesarea)
Gath-hepher
Sennabris
Philoteria
Homonœa
Emmatha
Gadara
Shimron
(Simonias)
NAZARETH
Daberath
(Dabarittha)
Mt. Tabor
1929
Japhia
(Japha)
Chesulloth
(Exaloth)
Gaba
Plain of Esdraelon
Sarid
En-dor

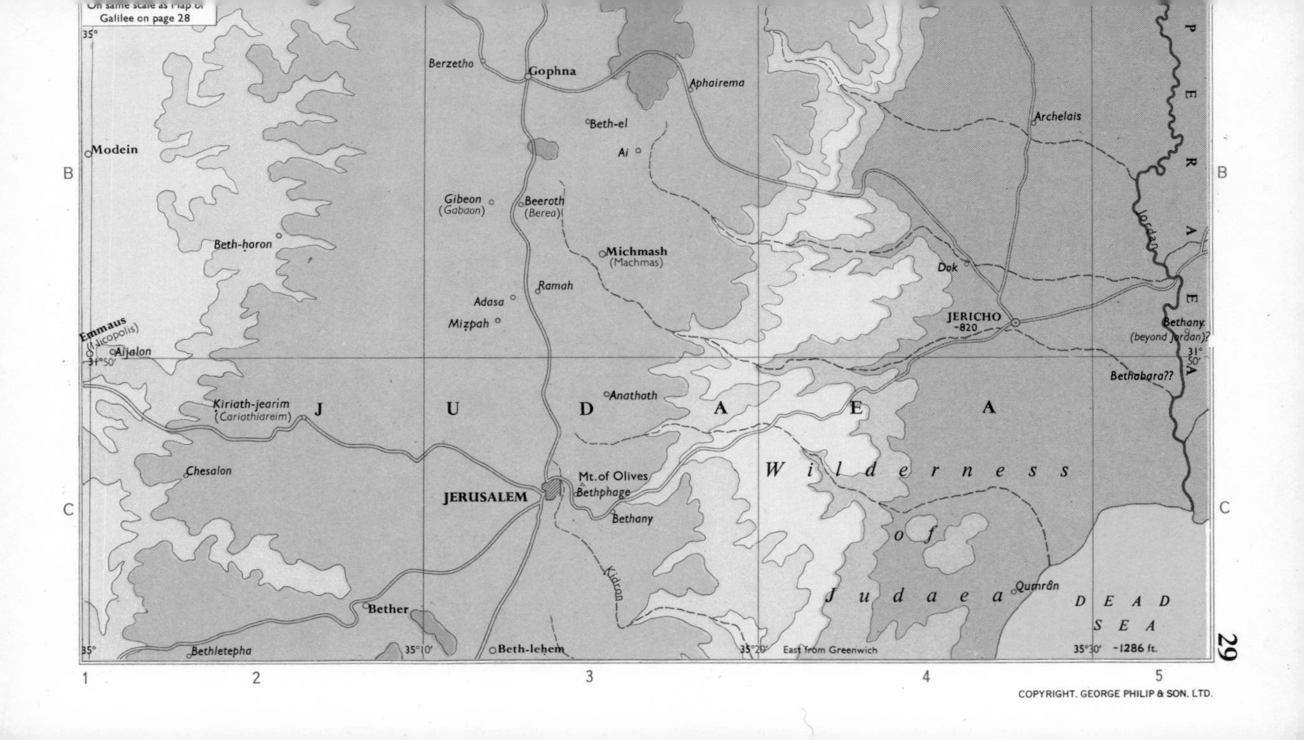
On same scale as Map of
Galilee on page 28
P E R A E A
Jordan
Bethany
(beyond Jordan)?
Bethabara??
Archelais
JERICHO
-820
Dok
Aphairema
Gophna
Berzetho
Beth-el
Ai
Modein
Gibeon
(Gabaon)
Beeroth
(Berea)
Michmash
(Machmas)
Beth-horon
Ramah
Adasa
Mizpah
Emmaus
Aijalon
Anathoth
Kiriath-jearim
(Cariathiareim)
J U D A E A
Chesalon
JERUSALEM
Mt. of Olives
Bethphage
Bethany
Kidron
Wilderness of Judaea
Qumrân
DEAD SEA
-1286 ft.
Bether
Beth-lehem
Bethletepha
35°
35°10′
35°20′
East from Greenwich
35°30′
31°50′
B
C
1
2
3
4
5
COPYRIGHT. GEORGE PHILIP & SON. LTD.

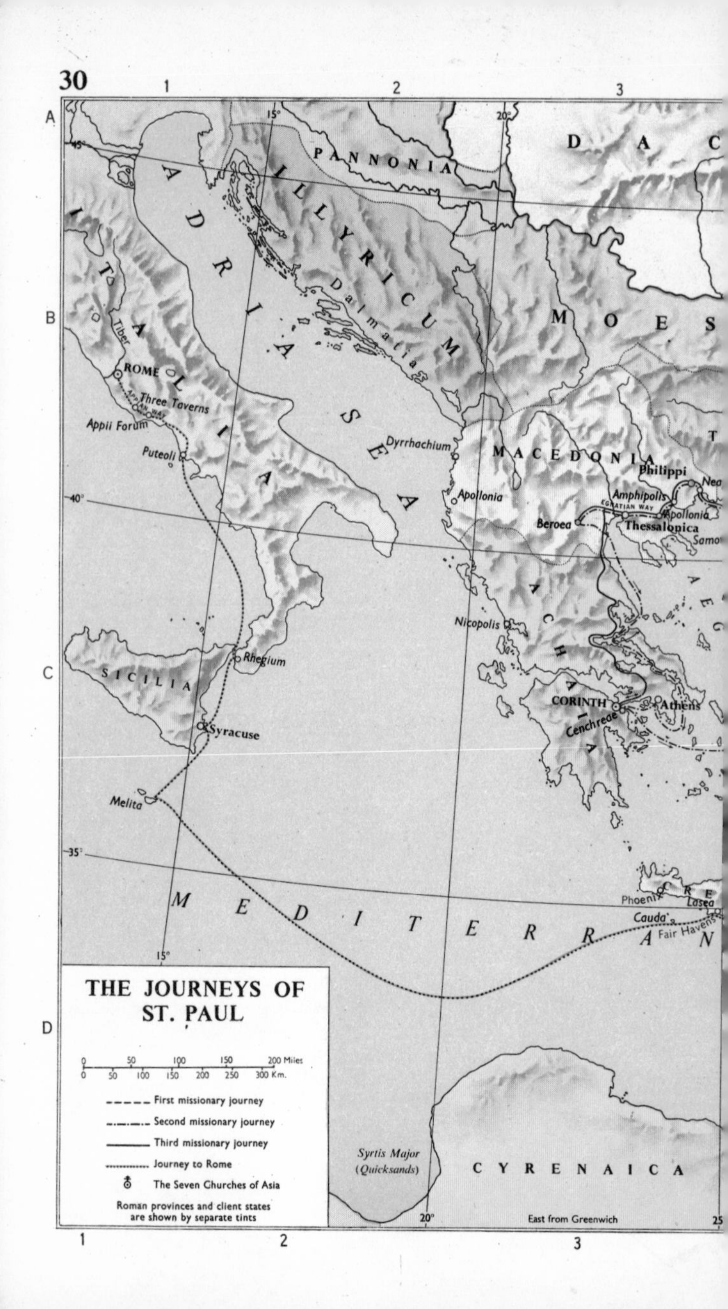
PANNONIA
ILLYRICUM
Dalmatia
ADRIA SEA
ITALIA
DACIA
MOESIA
MACEDONIA
ACHAIA
SICILIA
CYRENAICA
MEDITERRANEAN
Tiber
ROME
APPIAN WAY
Three Taverns
Appii Forum
Puteoli
Rhegium
Syracuse
Melita
Dyrrhachium
Apollonia
Philippi
Amphipolis
EGNATIAN WAY
Apollonia
Beroea
Thessalonica
Nicopolis
CORINTH
Cenchreae
Athens
Phoenix
Lasea
Cauda
Fair Havens
Syrtis Major
(Quicksands)
THE JOURNEYS OF ST. PAUL
0 50 100 150 200 Miles
0 50 100 150 200 250 300 Km.
First missionary journey
Second missionary journey
Third missionary journey
Journey to Rome
The Seven Churches of Asia
Roman provinces and client states are shown by separate tints
East from Greenwich

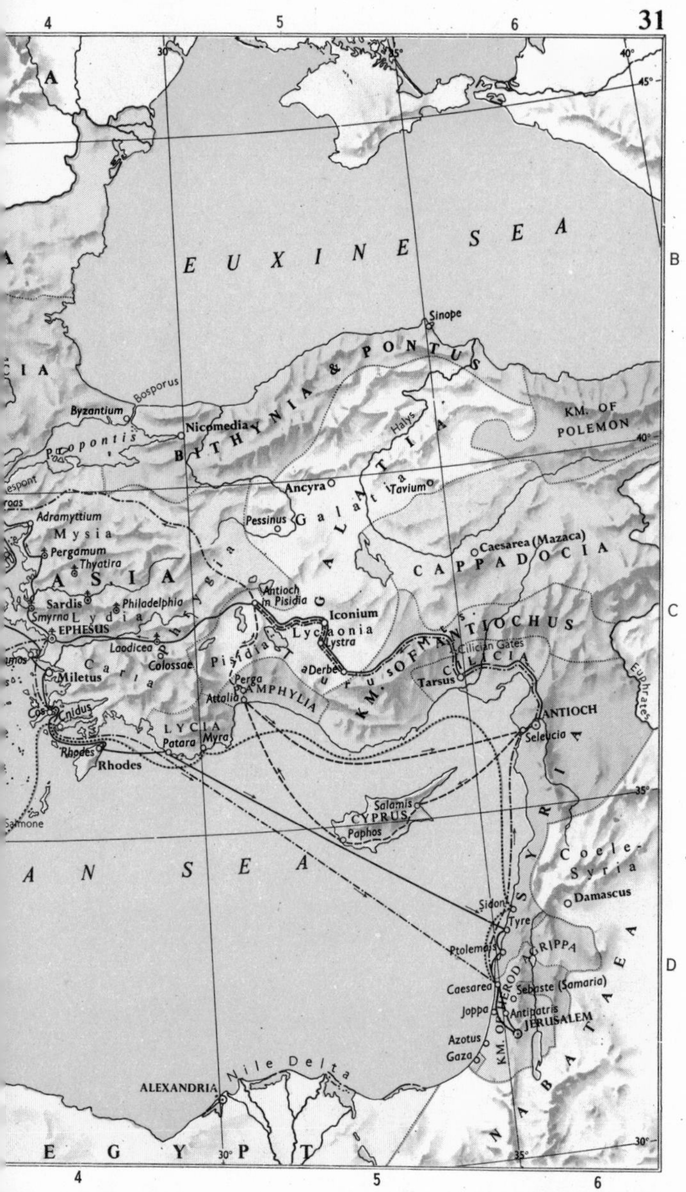
EUXINE SEA
Sinope
PONTUS
BITHYNIA & PONTUS
Bosporus
Byzantium
Nicomedia
Propontis
KM. OF POLEMON
Halys
GALATIA
Ancyra
Tavium
Pessinus
Galatia
Adramyttium
Mysia
Pergamum
Thyatira
ASIA
Sardis
Philadelphia
Smyrna
Lydia
EPHESUS
Phrygia
Antioch in Pisidia
Iconium
Lycaonia
Lystra
Derbe
CAPPADOCIA
Caesarea (Mazaca)
KM. OF ANTIOCHUS
Taurus Mts.
Cilician Gates
CILICIA
Tarsus
Laodicea
Colossae
Pisidia
Caria
Miletus
Perga
PAMPHYLIA
Attalia
Cos
Cnidus
LYCIA
Patara
Myra
Rhodes
ANTIOCH
Seleucia
Euphrates
SYRIA
Salamis
CYPRUS
Paphos
Salmone
SEA
Coele-Syria
Damascus
Sidon
Tyre
Ptolemais
KM. OF HEROD AGRIPPA
Caesarea
Sebaste (Samaria)
Joppa
Antipatris
JERUSALEM
Azotus
Gaza
NABATAEA
Nile Delta
ALEXANDRIA
EGYPT
COPYRIGHT. GEORGE PHILIP & SON. LTD.

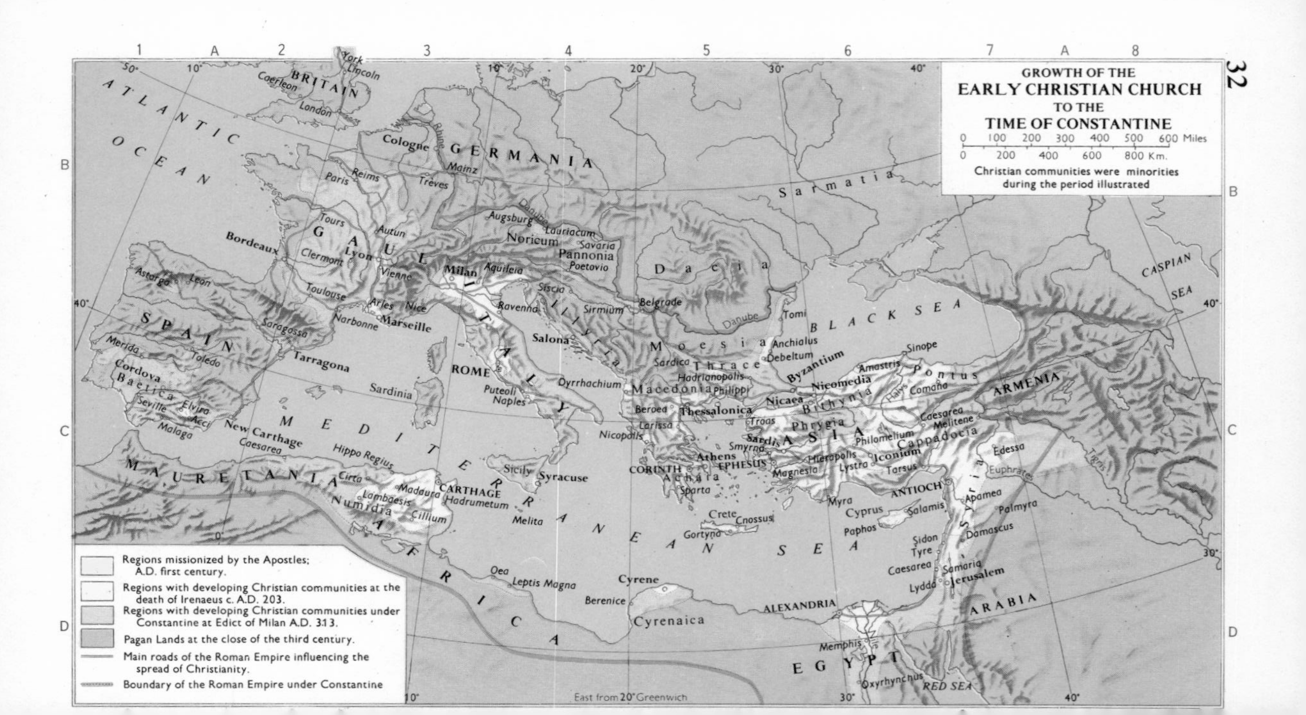
GROWTH OF THE
EARLY CHRISTIAN CHURCH
TO THE
TIME OF CONSTANTINE
0 100 200 300 400 500 600 Miles
0 200 400 600 800 Km.
Christian communities were minorities during the period illustrated
Regions missionized by the Apostles; A.D. first century.
Regions with developing Christian communities at the death of Irenaeus c. A.D. 203.
Regions with developing Christian communities under Constantine at Edict of Milan A.D. 313.
Pagan Lands at the close of the third century.
Main roads of the Roman Empire influencing the spread of Christianity.
Boundary of the Roman Empire under Constantine
East from 20° Greenwich
ATLANTIC OCEAN
BRITAIN
York
Lincoln
Caerleon
London
GERMANIA
Cologne
Rhine
Mainz
Treves
Reims
Paris
GAUL
Tours
Autun
Lyon
Clermont
Vienne
Bordeaux
Toulouse
Arles
Nice
Narbonne
Marseille
SPAIN
Astorga
Leon
Saragossa
Merida
Toledo
Tarragona
Cordova
Baetica
Seville
Elvira
Acci
Malaga
New Carthage
Caesarea
MAURETANIA
Hippo Regius
Cirta
Madaura
Lambaesis
Numidia
Cillium
CARTHAGE
Hadrumetum
AFRICA
Oea
Leptis Magna
MEDITERRANEAN SEA
Sardinia
ROME
Puteoli
Naples
ITALY
Milan
Aquileia
Ravenna
Sicily
Syracuse
Melita
Augsburg
Danube
Lauriacum
Noricum
Savaria
Pannonia
Poetovio
Siscia
Sirmium
Illyria
Salona
Dyrrhachium
Belgrade
Dacia
Sarmatia
Moesia
Sardica
Thrace
Hadrianopolis
Macedonia
Philippi
Beroea
Thessalonica
Larissa
Nicopolis
CORINTH
Achaia
Athens
Sparta
Crete
Cnossus
Gortyna
Cyrene
Berenice
Cyrenaica
Tomi
Anchialus
Debeltum
BLACK SEA
Byzantium
Nicomedia
Nicaea
Bithynia
Amastris
Sinope
Pontus
Halys
Comana
ARMENIA
Troas
Phrygia
Sardis
ASIA
Smyrna
EPHESUS
Magnesia
Hieropolis
Lystra
Philomelium
Iconium
Cappadocia
Caesarea
Melitene
Tarsus
ANTIOCH
Myra
Cyprus
Salamis
Paphos
Syria
Edessa
Euphrates
Tigris
Apamea
Palmyra
Damascus
Sidon
Tyre
Caesarea
Samaria
Jerusalem
Lydda
ARABIA
ALEXANDRIA
Memphis
EGYPT
Oxyrhynchus
RED SEA
CASPIAN SEA

Map References

ABBREVIATIONS

B. —Bay	I(s)—Island(s)	S.—Sea, South(ern)
C. —Cape	L. —Lake	V.—Valley
Des.—Desert	Mt.—Mount	W.—West(ern)
E. —East(ern)	N. —North(ern)	*W.—Wadi*
G. —Gulf	R. —River	*Kh.—Khirbet*

Identifications of sites are given in brackets where they are certain or reasonably probable. A ? is added only where there is a considerable degree of uncertainty.

An asterisk is prefixed to names to indicate that important excavations or archaeological finds have been made at the site mentioned.

Index